Tattvabodha

Tattvabodha

Essays from the Lecture Series of the National Mission for Manuscripts

Volume VI

Editor

V. Venkataraman Reddy

राष्ट्रीय पाण्डुलिपि मिशन
॥ विज्ञानमुपास्व ॥
National Mission for Manuscripts

Dev Publishers & Distributors

Published by:
National Mission for Manuscripts
11 Man Singh Road
New Delhi 110 001
Phone: 91 11 2307 3387
E-mail: directornamami@nic.in
Website: www.namami.nic.in

and Co-published by:
Dev Publishers & Distributors
2nd Floor, Prakash Deep,
22, Delhi Medical Association Road,
Darya Ganj, New Delhi - 110002
Phone: 91 11 43572647
Email: info@devbooks.co.in
Website: www.devbooks.co.in

ISBN 978-81-904029-4-1 (series)
ISBN 978-93-80829-46-3 (vol. VI)
First published 2017

Contents

Key to Transliteration

VOWELS

अ a	आ ā	इ i	ई ī	उ u	ऊ ū
(but)	(palm)	(it)	(beet)	(put)	(pool)
ऋ* ṛ	ॠ* ṝ	लृ* ḷ	ए e	ऐ ai	ओ o
			(play)	(air)	(toe)
	औ au				
	(loud)				

CONSONANTS

Guttural	क ka	ख kha	ग ga	घ gha	ङ ṅa
	(skate)	(blockhead)	(gate)	(ghost)	(sing)
Palatal	च ca	छ cha	ज ja	झ jha	ञ ña
	(chunk)	(catchhim)	(john)	(hedgehog)	(bunch)
Cerebral	ट ṭa	ठ ṭha	ड/ड़ ḍa	ढ/ढ़ ḍha	ण ṇa
	(start)	(anthill)	(dart)	(godhead)	
Dental	त ta	थ tha	द da	ध dha	न na
	(path)	(thunder)	(that)	(breathe)	(numb)
Labial	प pa	फ pha	ब ba	भ bha	म ma
	(spin)	(philosophy)	(bin)	(abhor)	(much)
Semi-vowels	य ya	र ra	ल la	ळ* ḷ	व va
	(young)	(drama)	(luck)		(vile)
Sibilants	श śa	ष ṣa	स sa	ह ha	
	(shove)	(bushel)	(so)	(hum)	

अं (—) *ṁ* or *ṃ amusūra* like *saṁskṛti/or soṃskṛti*

अः *visarga= ḥ*

ऽ *Avagraha* indicate elision of short vowel *a,* has no phonetic value.

*No exact English equivalents for these letters.

Foreword

In India, diverse knowledge traditions have emanated over centuries and the manuscripts are precious reserves of Indic knowledge systems. The National Mission for Manuscripts, in an attempt to disseminate the knowledge-content of these manuscipts, organizes the Tattvabodha Series of Lectures in Delhi and other parts of the country. In accordance with its title "Tattvabodha"-Awareness of Reality-the lecture series is intended to provide insights into different areas of knowledge by erudite scholars. The present Volume, sixth in the series, is a compilation of nine such discourses by eminent professors under Tattvabodha.

Prof. P. Sriramachandraidu, in his paper, has tried to justify that the antiquity of a work can be decided by the availability of many manuscripts with different readings and interpolations, also along with other factors. In his discussion, he also raised the question whether *Santarasa* should be considered as an independent primary *rasa* as accepted by Abhinavabharati, rather than as a component of the eight *rasas* of the Natyasastra.

Prof. G. C. Tripathi, in his article, has attempted to establish the importance of application of Prakrit in Sanskrit drama. Prakrit was the language of the common people. In his view, an appropriate use of Prakrit added vigor to the essence of drama.

In the article "Adhivedana", Prof. Radhavallabh Tripathi has taken us to the old scriptures to inform that the practice of "Divorce" was prevalent in ancient India. There were legitimate rules to deal with the outcome caused by the separation of husband and wife from each other due to various reasons.

Prof. B. N. Goswamy has opened our eyes to the contribution of Pandas, in his paper "Unsung Documents", which we had not paid attention to so far. The Pandas who serve at the places of pilgrimage are keepers of genealogy records of their clients. Prof. Goswamy had a first hand experience of how these records speak of our unknown past which may have long been lost due to passage of time.

Prof. Rama Nath Sharma's deliberation is a research on the "knowledge" as represented by the rules of Sanskrit grammar. He attempts to clarify that the rules of grammar are formulated for capturing the nature of usage, not to dictate the reality of usage. A grammarian does not have any control over the goal of his analysis.

Prof. Dipak Bhattachaya's article has focussed on two words - "kanva" and "krnva". He has delved deep into linguistics, mythology, literature and grammar to decipher the probable implications of those two words through derivations and usages.

Prof. Ashok Kumar Goswami has presented Anundoram Borooah, the pioneer orientalist and a great scholar of the nineteenth century. He has enlightened us with Borooah's contribution in Indology.

Prof. S. P. Verma's paper tries to convey that Persian paintings tell the story of India's cultural past. They played an important role in influencing the history of art in India.

Prof. Peter M. Scharf, in his elaborate paper has attempted to take manuscripts of yesteryears and knowledge-content of our ancestors to the digital age. Prof. Scharf has rightly mentioned that the knowledge exists fundamentally in the consciousness of knowledgeable people and "New Media" provides technological advances that contribute new possibilities for propagation of that knowledge.

This Tattvabodha volume, with contributions from renowned scholars in their respective fields, seeks to make a contribution to the dissimination of knowledge to interested readers. On behalf of the Mission, I, wholeheartedly thank the scholars for their contributions and my thanks also goes to M/S Dev Publishers & Distributors for bringing out this volume. It would not be out of place to mention that the opinions expressed by the individual scholars in their respective papers are their own and the Mission does not take responsibility of expression of their viewpoints.

V. Venkataramana Reddy
Director,
National Mission for Manuscripts

1

Rasādhyāya of Naṭyaśāstra with Abhinava Bhārati

P. Sriramachandrudu

THERE ARE HUNDREDS OF old Sanskrit works on various subjects which have come down to us through oral tradition for some time, through handwritten manuscripts after some time and through print in later times. Almost all of them contain different readings, interpolations and lacunae in many places. It is an arduous task for the editors of these works to identify interpolations, fill up the missing words or sentences and to fix the correct readings. Many commentators of ancient times had successfully undertaken this task and tried to give us texts with correct readings applying their own methods.

During the last hundred and fifty years of period many works like Kavyas, Dramas, Epics, Purāṇas and Śāstric works were edited by scholars and they were published giving only the readings fixed by the editors without any indication of variations in readings. But some publishers like the Ānandasrama Mudranālaya of Poona gave different readings, (पाठान्तर s) in the foot notes which were quite helpful to the readers who look for better readings

The efforts of some of the Western Scholars in collecting, preserving and editing the old manuscripts, is no doubt highly admirable. But many Mahārajas of different Principalities and States in India have been maintaining big libraries with very valuable collections as their pious duty, but for whose zeal for the preservation of Indian literary traditions and culture, nothing could have been done by the scholars of recent times.

Many critical editions of various works are brought out by many Indian scholars who worked with perseverance and real love for the promotion of knowledge. The critical edition of Mahābhārata published by the Bhandarkar Oriental Research Institute, Poona and of the Vālmīki Rāmāyaṇa brought out by the Oriental Research Institute of Baroda are well known. it is a matter of pride for all of us connected with the Osmania University that our colleague in the University Dr. Kaluri Hanumanta Rao, Professor of Chemical Engineering has published recently a critical edition of Rāmāyaṇa, over which he worked for about thirty years.

An edition of Śrīmadbhāgavata also was published by the Trirumala Tirupati Devastanam.

As I feel the antiquity or otherwise of a work can be decided by the availability of many manuscripts with different readings and interpolations also along with other factors. In the first meeting of the Bhagavata Project Committee I told them, Bhāgavatam being a Purāṇa of recent times, twelfth or thirteenth century A.D. many manuscripts of ancient times might not be available for study, to justify the name of critical edition. Ultimately it was published with three commentaries following the Advaita, Viśiṣṭādvaita and Dvaita traditions.

It is interesting to see that even some of the very important works like the Mahābhāshya of Patanjali were completely lost in some parts of the country for centuries and were retrieved from some remote places. It is said at the end of the second Kāṇḍa of *Vākyapadīya* that Mahābhāṣya was practically driven out from North India for a very long time and was restored by the efforts of scholars like चन्द्राचार्य from a far away place in South:

"कृतेऽथ पतञ्जलिना गुरुणा तत्त्वदर्शिना ।
सर्वेषां" न्यायबीजानां महाभाष्ये निबन्धने ॥ (वा.प.2.177)

बैजिसौभवहर्यक्षैः शुष्कतर्कानुसारिभिः ।
आर्षे विप्लाविते ग्रन्थे संग्रहप्रतिकञ्चुके ॥

यः पतञ्जलिशिष्येभ्यो भ्रष्टो व्याकरणागमः ।
काले स दाक्षिणात्येषु ग्रन्थमात्रे व्यवस्थितः ॥

पर्वतादागमं लब्ध्वा भाष्यबीजानुसारिभिः ।
स नीतो बहुशाखात्त्वं चन्द्राचार्यादिभिः पुनः ॥ (वा प. 2. 179,180)

This is the reason why it is maintained by scholars that Mahābhāṣya as it is available now is mutilated and incomplete and is full of lacunae, which make some passages difficult to understand.

The great philosopher poet, Sri Harsha of twelfth century indicates in his *Naishadhiya Charitam* that some portions of Mahābhāṣya, the purport of which cannot be properly appreciated were put in brackets (कुण्डली) by old scholars and they are inaccessible, like the city of Vidarbha which is surrounded by a big moat परिखा--

परिखावलयच्छलेन या न परेषां ग्रहणस्य गोचरा ।
फणिभाषितभाष्यफक्किकाविषमा कुण्डलनामवापिता । (नै. च. 2.95)

Now coming to our times, *Sangita-Candra*, a treatise on Nāṭya Śāstra by Śuklapandita which was taken from South to Kashmir, by Jagajjyoti, the king of Kashmir was brought to South by Sri Manavalli Ramakrishna Kavi and was published by the Sanskrit Academy, Osmania University in 1982.

It so happened- when the Academy was struggling for existence due to lack of funds Dr. P. S. R. Appa Rao, the then Director of Cultural Affairs, Government of A. P. gave a manuscript copy of the above book to the then Director of the Academy, that was myself, with the suggestion that it might be published by the Academy, being a very rare and unpublished book. He also told me that it was found by Sri Ramakrishna Kavi in the library of H. H. The Maharaja of Nepal on 2-4-1940, which was presented to Dr. Appa Rao by Sri Kavi with a request to get it published somewhere or other. I edited and managed to publish it for the Academy in 1982. At the end of the manuscript there are two and half slokas.

सन्ति यद्यपि भूयांसो ग्रन्था: संगीतगोचरा: ।
तथापीदृशमन्यत्तु नास्तीति परिचिन्तयन् ॥
पीयूषहरणं तार्क्ष्यो यद्वाद्विहितवान्यथा ।
तथैतत्पुस्तकं श्लाध्यं दूराद्यक्षिणदेशत: ।
आजहार नृपश्रेष्ठ: श्रीजगज्ज्योतिरीशिता ॥ (सं. च. 8.268)

I dedicated this work to Sri Ramakrishna Kavi, whom I did not have the opportunity of ever seeing, and wrote:

सन्ति यद्यपि भूयांसो ग्रन्था: संगीतगोचरा: ।
तथापीदृशमन्यत्तु नास्तीति परिचिन्तयन् ॥
पीयूषहरणं तार्क्ष्यो यद्वाद्विहितवान्यथा ।
तथैतत्पुस्तकं श्लाध्यं दूरान्नेपालदेशत: ॥
प्रत्याहरन्मानवल्लि रामकृष्णकवि: पुरा ॥

Though the manuscript was in a good condition there were many scribal errors which stood in the way of understanding the meaning. Such places I had tried to correct with the help of the *Nāṭyaśāstra, Saṅgītaratnākara* and *Nṛttaratnāvali*. When a complete line appeared corrupt, line in similar context from some of these works was given in the foot-note.

The Nāṭyaśāstra of Bharata which, according to many scholars may be placed in the second century B.C. and its commentary Abhinava Bhāratī by Abhinavagupta of the tenth or eleventh century A.D. both defy the efforts of scholars to arrive at correct readings. We have to be content with surmises and assumptions regarding them. When we can understand why there should be so much of confusion about the correct text of Nāṭyaśāstra which is a very old work. Even the Abhinavabhāratī is full of wrong readings and many lacunae, ग्रन्थपात's

It may be noted, when many manuscripts of other literary works of the same period found in other parts of the country are relatively free from some of the defects, only the works from Kashmir are generally full of such defects. Almost all the important works on Alankāra-Śāstra were authorred by the Kashmirian scholars and all of them compete with each other in this aspect. This is on account of invasions of foreigners who did not spare the libraries from distruction. This is the reason generally given by some people. But it was a common problem faced by the whole country.

The only plausible reason appears to be, subject to the correction by the manuscriptologists present here, the material used by those people for writing like the Bhurja bark etc., must be inferior to the Tala-Patra used in other parts of the country.

The only exception appears to be the Kāvylāṅkārasūtra vṛtti of Vāmana. In my humble opinion Vāmana, the author of this work might be different from Vāmana who is said to have flourished in the court of Jayāpīḍa, a Kashmirian ruler; because, unlike all the Ālaṅkārikas of Kashmir who accept only three guṇās, Vamana accepts ten guṇās like many of the Southern Ālaṅkārikas.

The text of Nāṭyaśāstra was first published in the Nirṇayasāgar Press, Bombay, in the year 1920; and in 1929 by the Choukhamba Press, Banaras.

Sri Manavalli Ramakrishna Kavi of Tirupati edited Nāṭyaśāstra along with the commentary Abhinavabharati and the same was published in four volumes in the Gaekwad Oriental Series, and the first volume appeared in the year 1929. Another work of Sri Kavi is भरतकोश, a stupendous work.

As was stated by Sri Ramakrishna Kavi in his introduction to the second volume of Nāṭyaśāstra, he consulted 40 manuscripts of Nāṭyaśāstra and found none of them fully agreeing with the other. He felt there must have been two recensions of Nāṭyaśāstra, one Northern recension and the other Southern recension. Some scholars do not accept this theory of two recensions.

This textual confusion is found in the whole of Nāṭyaśāstra and the commentary through out the sixth chapters, Rasādhyāya contains very important differences in readings especially pertaining to the Śānta Rasa.

Rasa is introduced by Bharata for the first time and that too as an important element pertaining to Rupaka only though it is given importance in Śravya kāvyas also by later rhetoricians.

For a long time Rasas were only eight in number. The original text of Bharata's Nāṭyaśāstra mentions only eight-Rasas-

शृङ्गारहास्यकरुणरौद्रवीरभयानकाः ।
बीभत्साद्भुतसंज्ञौचेत्यष्टौ नाट्ये रसाः स्मृताः । (ना.शा- VI-15)

The earlier poets also were speaking only of eight Rasas. Kalidasa says in *Vikramorvasiya*-

मुनिना भरतेन यःप्रयोगो भवतीष्वष्टरसाश्रयो नियुक्तः ।
ललिताभिनयं तमद्य भर्ता मरुतां द्रष्टुमनाः सलोकपालः ॥ (II-18)

Vararuchi, mentions only eight Rasas, in his भाण उभयाभिसारिका । Thus only eight Rasas appear to be known to Bharata. But the Śānta rasa must have been introduced by later writers who accordingly amended the readings in Nāṭyaśāstra which was taken as the authority of Abhinava Gupta who being a philosopher is very much interested in accepting Śānta as an important Rasa, so important for him as to be accepted as the प्रकृतिरस of all the other Rasas.

After commenting on the passages of Nāṭyaśāstra which speak of only eight Rasas he writes-

''अथ शान्तो नाम शमस्थायिभावात्मको मोक्षप्रवर्तकः''
''तथा च चिरन्तनपुस्तकेषु स्थायिभावान् रसत्वमुपनेष्यामः'' इत्यनन्तरम्-
''शान्तो नाम शमस्थायिभावात्मकः'' इत्यादि शान्तलक्षणं पठ्यते ।

Starting with this statement Abhinavagupta argues vehemently by that Śānta also can be given a very important place in a drama as can be found in dramas like Nāgānanda.

Regarding the स्थायिभाव of शान्त he introduced the views of some writers who accept शम and refutes them. There were some writers, quoted by Abhinava who accepted निर्वेद as स्थायिभाव। Abhinava feels that only तत्त्वज्ञान can be स्थायिन् of शान्त while निर्वेद could be its व्यभिचारिभाव ततश्च तत्त्वज्ञानमेवेदं तत्त्वज्ञानमालया परिपोष्यमाणमिति न निर्वेदः स्थायी, किन्तु तत्त्वज्ञानमेव स्थायी भवेत्। यत्तु व्यभिचारिव्याख्यानावसरे वक्ष्यते तच्चिरकालविभ्रमविप्रलब्धस्य उपादेयत्वनिवृत्तये यत् सम्यग् ज्ञानम्, यथा-

वृथा दुग्धोऽनड्वान् स्तनभरनता गौरिति परं
परिष्वक्तः षण्डो युवतिरिति लावण्यरहितः ।
कृता वैदूर्याशा विकचकिरणे काचशकले
मया मूढेन त्वां कपणमगुणज्ञं प्रणमता ॥

इति तन्निर्वेदस्य खेदरूपस्य विभावत्वेन। एतच्च तत्रैव वक्ष्यामः - (ना.शा. Part I.p.330. Parimal Publications)

It may be stated here-Śānta may be an independent Rasa. But it is a Rasa which can be fully developed and appreciated only in a Śravya Kavya. That is the reason why Anandavardhana has accepted Śānta as the main Rasa in Mahabharata as he states-

महाभारतेऽपि शास्त्ररूपकाव्यच्छायान्वयिनि वृष्णिपाडवविरसावसानवैमनस्यदायिनीं समाप्ति मुपनिबध्नता महामुनिना वैराग्यजननतात्पर्यं प्राधान्येन स्वप्रबन्धस्य दर्शयता मोक्षलक्षणः पुरुषार्थः शान्तो रसश्च मुख्यतया विवक्षाविषयत्वेन सूचितः ...

स्वयमेव चैतदुद्गीर्णं तेन उदीर्णमहामोहमग्नमुज्जिहीर्षता लोकम् अतिविमलज्ञानालोक दायिना लोकनाथेन-

यथा यथा विपर्येति लोकतन्त्रमसारवत् ।
तथा तथा विरागोऽत्र जायते नात्र संशयः ॥

इत्यादि बहुशः कथयता। (ध्व.आ. p. 530)

Taking the clue from this statement of Anandavardhana, one may accept Śānta rasa in works like रघुवंश also which end with the narration of an unhappy end of the Raghuvansa.

But to give an important place as Angirasa in Rupakas also may be against our experiences. There might be a flash of Santarasa in dramas like Nagananda which should be taken as an Anga of Sṛngāra or Dānavīra in that drama.

Therefore Dhananjaya and Dhanika who oppose the prominence of Śānta in Drama appear to be practical in their approach so far as drama is concerned. "शममपि केचित् प्राहुः पुष्टिर्नाट्येषु नैतस्य" (द.रू. IV. 35) Says Dhananjaya.

But Dhanika, the commentator on Daśarūpaka does not accept Śānta rasa even in a श्रव्यकाव्य। He says that such a state as शम is the very negation of the possibility of affirming anything of it. For, whatever way in which we can describe it is incorrect in so far as we are always describing in worldly terms something which is not like anything of this world. The Upanishads themselves describe the Brahman by saying that "it is not this, not this. Such a state can never be made a subject of Kavya even."

शान्तो हि तावत्-

''न यत्र दुःखं न सुखं न चिन्ता न द्वेषरागौ न च काचिदिच्छा ।

रसस्तु शान्तः कथितो मुनीन्द्रैः सर्वेषु भावेषु शमप्रधानः''

इत्येवंलक्षणः। तदा तस्य मोक्षावस्थायामेव आत्मस्वरूपापत्तिलक्षणायां प्रादुर्भावात् तस्य च स्वरूपेण अनिर्वचनीयता । तथा हि श्रुतिरपि 'स एष नेति नेति' इत्यन्यापोहरूपेणाह (द. रू. p.124)

In view of these different views मध्यमार्ग appears to be good. Though it is not possible to maintain Śānta Rasa throughout a play as an अङ्गिरस it can be maintained so in a Śravya Kavya with Nirveda as स्थायिभाव but not तत्त्वज्ञान as proposed by Abhinava. This is the reason, inspite of Abhinava's opposition Mammaṭa accepts निर्वेद as स्थायिन् of Śānta. After listing eight Rasās he says-

निर्वेदस्थायिभावोऽस्ति शान्तोऽपि नवमो रसः।

By making a separate statement regarding शान्तरस as the ninth Rasa he indicates that he is in favour accepting Śānta as Rasa but as pertaining to श्रव्यकाव्य and we may agree with him.

2

The Role and Function of Prakrit in the Sanskrit Drama

G. C. Tripathi

Uniqueness of Drama:

IT WAS A GREAT SURPRISE for Sir William Jones, a judge at the Calcutta High Court and later the celebrated founder of the Asiatic Society of Bengal, who was learning Sanskrit from a Bengali Pandit around 1780 or so, with the purpose of having a first hand recourse to the Sanskrit Dharmashāstric literature, when he learned from his Guru that Sanskrit is not limited to the legal works only but contains also *belle lettre*, fine literature, including beautiful *dramas*. That 'Hindus' have also composed dramatic works in their 'religious' language was a big surprise for him, since he was taught in his courses at the Oxford University that among the old people, it were only the Greeks who developed this particular genre of literature. So after finishing his study of *Manusmriti* and translating it into English, he devoted himself fully to the study of Kalidasa's Shakuntalam and produced a wonderful translation of it which introduced the Sanskrit drama to the west and, as is well known, won the accolades of such great litterateur as Goethe.

Origin of Drama:

European Indologist, who mostly came to Sanskrit after having a thorough training in Greek and Latin, very often tended in favour of assigning greater antiquity to drama in Greece and were of the opinion that the drama became known to India after the settlement of Greeks in the North-West of this country after the invasion of Alexander. Sanskrit word *yavanikā* (curtain) which can yield the sense of 'something belonging to the yavanas' was cited by Albrecht Weber as a sure proof for establishing the indebtedness of Indian drama to the Greek one.

Although it was pointed out by some that the Greek drama, enacted in an amphitheatre did not have a curtain at all, the argument held good for a long time. The best explanation of this word according to me is to trace its origin to the Vedic root *yu* meaning 'to separate' (cf. *divānaktam śarum asmad yuyotam*, RV 7.71.1, *yuyodhi asmad juhurāṇam enas*...RV 1.189.1); *yāvanam* = separation, '*Yavanikā*', therefore should be a device which separated the spectators from the stage, an etymology which deserves serious consideration by the scholars. In any case, the theory of the Greek origin of Indian drama seems now to have been finally discarded; to quote F.B.J. Kuiper (*Varuṇa and Vidūṣaka: On the Origin of Sanskrit Drama* (Amsterdam 1979): "The old ideas of a Greek origin and that of Greek-Roman pantomime being the source of the Indian drama have definitely been refuted". Same is the case with the theories seeking its origin in shadow plays (*vayang*) or puppet theatre (both of which are believed to have originated in India) proposed by Sten Konow and Pischel respectively.

Much before Kuiper, A. B. Keith in his "Sanskrit drama" had examined the theory at length and had come to the conclusion that because of a very different nature of Greek drama and its stage, the origin of Indian drama must be sought in the symbolic rites and gestures constituting the Vedic sacrifice. It is true that a Vedic sacrifice is nothing but a *Rūpaka* which symbolically represents or re-creates a certain cosmic event. When the priest, for example, in a particular sacrifice makes three strides on a tiger hide, the text equates him with Viṣṇu who in his giant form, covered the three worlds becoming master of them. Black hair on the hide, according to the text (ŚB) denote night and bright hair the day. The priest thus on behalf of the sacrificer conquers both space and time and becomes master of them.

One can even go a step further and show that a number of religious rites which form part of the Vedic sacrifices have actually been taken from the believes, practices and ceremonies prevalent in those times among the common people in the society which were later made sacerdotal. Take for example the rite of purchasing and bargaining the price of Soma plant in the Somayāga or Agniṣtoma which looks like a dramatic scene in itself. A strong act of haggling takes place just outside the marked boundary of the sacred space; the Soma seller demands more, the priests offer less and increase it bit by bit till at last a cow is conceded to the vendor which is also his original demand. The whole act presents a dramatic scene that has been picked up from a number of such bargaining scenes which one encounters daily in the Indian markets. This profane act is then brought into the religions sphere and converted into a compulsory sacerdotal rite forming part of an important sacrifice.

The fact that the first ever play was enacted with the help of gods and the nymphs during the greatest and the most popular religious festival of Indradhvaja (NS 1.54), various gods were placed on the different parts of the theatre for its protection and that before the beginning of the play a quasi religious ceremony in the form of *Pūrvaranga* was performed, followed by musical presentation by a verse (Nāndī) seeking the blessing of some god also indicate towards its religious origin and character.

The so called 'dialogue hymns' of the RV like that of *Purūravā* and *Urvaśī* and '*Yama-Yamī*' etc. with no prose piece joining the verses and which according to S. Levi and L. v. Schroeder etc. were to be supplied *ad hoc* by the priests each time may be considered as a part of some sacrificial drama played by priests as a fragmentary part of some major religious ritual of which the prose pieces have not been preserved for us.

It is our common mistake to believe that the Vedas are the oldest sources of our culture, that our culture *starts* from the Vedas and that nothing was there before them. But in fact, they might have emerged much later. Their content betrays that they came into being when the Indian culture had attained quite a high water mark and the religious rites mentioned in them were formed taking note of the believes of common folk as their primeval source and many rites of the sacrifice also were inspired by activities taking place in folk functions and festivals.

The second obvious source of Indian drama is dance, especially folk dances of ancient India. Because of a sizable number of inherent dramatic and emotional elements, postures, facial expressions and gestures (*mudrās*) described in detail by Bharata in the NS and freely made use of in the dramas, there is full justification of accepting dance as a precursor and one of the sources of the classical drama.

The fact is also strengthened by the etymology of a number of words connected with the art of drama like *nāṭaka* or *nāṭikā* (drama), *nāṭyam* (dramatic performance), *naṭa* (the actor) etc. which go back to the root *naṭ, a* Prakrit descendent of the Sanskrit root *nṛt* = to dance. In Indian tradition of fine arts and literature, dance and drama are regarded as inseparable from each other and are treated together in the works of dramaturgy. The Nāṭyaśāstra of Bharata is a reference work not only for the dramatists but also for the dancers and that perhaps to a higher degree.

However the dance form which might have served as inspiration or even source of Indian drama might have been simple, folk dance and not any embellished classical dance form. Folk dances are part of every culture, even of forest tribes, and are natural expressions of joy on the occasions of festivals, marriages and at harvesting seasons. They have existed since the earliest times of the formation of human societies. A number of folk elements form part of the Indian drama, which point towards its close connection with the folk.

So also are a number of folk elements which form part of our Sanskrit drama. Without these elements a drama cannot have a normal and natural *worldly* character; cannot be a *"bhāvānukīrtanam"* (NS 1.107), *'lokavṛttānukaraṇam'* (NS 1.112) or *"avasthānukṛti"*—"the re-production or re-creation of a given situation or an event" which is actually the definition of drama given by our dramaturgists. In spite of the claim of Bharata, therefore, that the drama has been created by god Brahmā by joining together the four elements taken from the four Vedas, viz. the plot of the story or the text, from the Ṛgveda, music from the Sāmaveda, performance from the Yajurveda and its *Rasas* (the sentiments etc.) — the main ingredient of drama — from the Atharvaveda (NS 1.17); the '*loka*' element in the drama is very strong otherwise it may not be acceptable to the common viewers. Excerpts taken exclusively from the Vedas can only create a 'mystery play' like we have in Christianity; the 'passion plays' depicting the last days or the final day of the life of Christ, but not a play which pleases the general public.

The chief purpose of the drama according to Bharata is *lokānurañjana* (NS 1.120); to provide relief and entertainment to the common folk. It is a piece of art which entertains and provides solace to the common people, and to those poor souls (*tapasvins*) who are suffering from grief (*duḥkhārta*), are despondent due to adversities facing them (*śokārta*) or who are exhausted after having toiled the whole day (*śramārta*):

> दु:खार्तानां श्रमार्तानां शोकार्त्तानां तपस्विनाम्।
> विश्रान्तिजननं काले नाट्यमेतद् भविष्यति॥ (NS 1.114)

Since it is clear that the drama combines in itself both Veda and Loka, it is quite understandable and justified that it should make use of both the languages current at that time: Sanskrit for the elite and Prakrit for the common folk for their entertainment as well as edification.

All the classical forms of art, whether music, painting, sculptures, performing arts and even literature have their origin in folk which attains its gradual refinement in the hands of connoisseures and becomes 'classical'. It is therefore not improbable that like many folk forms of plays like Jātrās. Svāng or Nauṭankī etc. some form of folk drama might have been prevalent among the common masses which inspired certain rites even in the Vedic ritual like Mahāvrata in which a particular rite foresees conversation between a Brahmacharī and a courtesan. And if we accept this theory of the popular and folk origin of Indian drama, it is obvious that the dialogues in such a folk theatre must not have been in the polished and chaste Vedic or Brahmanical Sanskrit but surely in Prakrit, and if this be true than we even have to postulate that the so called 'Sanskrit drama' was actually, ab origine, entirely in Prakrit, in an unwritten form which later, in its literary form, was rendered partly in Sanskrit with introduction of the dialogues of the members of the higher strata of the society along with insertion of verses depicting emotional situations and the like, perhaps under the influence of the oral presentations of the epics and may be also Purāṇas which were common in those days.

Probable Date of the emergence of Sanskrit Drama:

Although the words Śailūṣha which later means a 'theatre artist' appears already in the Yajurveda (VS, Ch. 30) and this as well as the word Naṭa appear in the Mbh. and Rām. etc., further, a work named *'Naṭasūtra by Śilālin'* is mentioned in the Ashtadhyāyī of Panini, besides the dramatist *Kṛśāśva*, and the existence of the plays *'Kansavadha'* and *'Balibandhanam'* is attested by Patanjali in his Mahābhāṣya (150 B.C.), yet it is difficult to say when exactly the Sanskrit drama attained its fully developed form to the extent as we find it around the beginning of the Christian era in the works of Ashvaghosha and even Kalidasa, if we place him in the 1st c. BC and who again makes a mention of three of his illustrious predecessors (Bhāsa, Saumilla and Kaviputra).

Very near to the time of Ashvaghosha i.e. around the beginning of the Christian era or a little before (2nd BC–2nd AD) a wonderful compendium of dramaturgy is compiled by some anonymous author who passes it under the name of Bharata who is said to have received this Śāstra (discipline) directly from the creator god Brahmā himself. It is a veritable encyclopaedia of dance, drama, music and poetry and is more in extent than the works 'Poetics" and 'Aesthetics' of Aristotle taken together. It gives a comprehensive and rich picture of the classical Indian theatre in its fully developed form: ten types of plays (*rūpaka*) with an eleventh derivative type (*nāṭikā*), three types of stages (square, oblong and triangular), way of the composition of the plays including the indications of the different types of language and dialects of Prakrit to be spoken by different types of characters, its sentiments and aesthetics, way of speaking and dialogue delivery, ways of acting, bodily gestures, make-up, production, presentation, qualities of spectators and music to be employed in various situations etc. etc.

Such a work as Nāṭyaśāstra presupposes existence of a rich literature because it can only be compiled when sufficient number of dramatic works are available and are in free circulation. We may therefore postulate a date for the beginning of Sanskrit drama somewhere around 10th–8th c. BC otherwise the composition of a 'Naṭasūtra' till the time of Pāṇini is not possible. That the origin of Indian drama goes back to the latest phase of Vedic literature (10th-8th c. BC.) is also proved by the accented Vedic text of the Suparṇādhyāya (published by NMM) which is in fact a perfect dramatic text in metrical form.

The Buddhist Ashvaghosha is usually considered by the Westerners as the first dramatist whose works have survived for us, although only in broken pieces of a palmleaf manuscript discovered in the desert of Turfan. His date is historically fixed as he was a contemporary of Kanishka, the probably founder of Shaka era (which starts in 78 AD). Fragments of three of his dramas have been discovered from Turfan one of which is *Shāriputra-prakaraṇa* or *Shāradvatīputraprakaraṇa* composed by—as the colophon says—Ashvaghosha, the son of Suvarṇākshī. The titles of other two are not known although their fragments are available. The Prakaraṇa is one of the ten (or more) varieties of Sanskrit drama which is the most extensive of all and can have upto 10 acts. The Prakaraṇa of Ashvaghosha has nine acts. This drama is in no way different or more primitive than the later Prakaraṇas like *Mṛchhakaṭika*, or *Mālatīmādhava* in composition, plot construction or any other dramatic devices found in later works. The dialogues are both in Sanskrit and Prakrit depending upon the characters, with verses in Sanskrit. It presents before us a fully developed and fine form of a Sanskrit–Prakrit drama and follows closely most of the rules laid down by Bharata in the Nāṭyaśāstra regarding the overall structure of the drama.

Bharata lays down specific rules as regards the use of the languages and dialects in the dramas (NS 17.25–27). He first divides the language into four categories : 1. *Atibhāṣā* i.e. the language of gods and the ancient Vedic Rishis, 2. *Ārya bhāṣā*, i.e. the refined and polished classical Sanskrit spoken by kings etc.. 3. *Jātibhāṣā*, i.e. the natural regional language of all the four *varṇas* or the common masses which is further divided into Sanskrit and Prakrit, 4. The fourth is the language of non-human beings like birds and animals which is imitated as per requirement during the performance (*Yonyantarī*).

Sanskrit is to be normally spoken by the heroes of the play who are allowed to converse in Prakrit, if need be, according to situation. However if they are in an adverse situation, have turned pauper or are totally inebriated, they must not speak Sanskrit but only Prakrit. Kings, Princes and occasionally also queens speak Sanskrit. (NS 17.31–32).

Sages, Vedic scholars, priests, learned people, students and itinerant preachers with special marks of their school or sect should also be made to speak Sanskrit. Courtesan usually speak Prakrit but may use Sanskrit while talking about art and literature with learned people of refined taste.

The nymphs usually speak Sanskrit due to their association with gods but may speak Prakrit when moving on earth among the mortals. (17.43)

Prakrit is spoken by women and children in general, always by the jester (*Viduṣaka*), by all monks belonging to Buddhist, Ājīvaka and Jaina faith as well as by labourers, persons belonging to the lower strata of the society as well as persons of bad characters like thieves, robbers and outcastes. (NS 33–36)

Bharata enumerates seven varieties or dialects of Prakrit which are: Māgadhī, Ardha Māgadhī, Prācyā, Śaurasenī, Avantijā, Dākṣinātyā and Vahḷīkā. Māgadhī was the language of Rajagriha-Pataliputra upto western part of Bengal, Ardhamāgadhī belongs to the region of western Bihar i.e. from Bhojpur upto Varanasi, Prācyā is spoken in Dakṣiṇa Pānchāl—from Kannauj to Varanasi, whereas Shaurasenī was spoken in the large area comprising Vraja and Śūrasena which today forms western U.P., Estern Rajasthan and Hariana. Vāhlīkī is spoken in Afghanistan and Bactria, Avantijā in the Malwa region and the Dākṣinātyā covers the languages of the entire Dakṣiṇāpatha. Bharata strongly recommends that the normal Prakrit of prose conversation ought to be Śauraseni only. (शौरसेनं समाश्रित्य भाषा कार्या तु नाटके, 17-46)

Nature of Prakrit in Sanskrit dramas :

What is striking here is the fact that Mahārāṣṭrī, the most celebrated among the Prakrit and the language of the Prakrit lyrics as well as of the Mahākāvyas, is nowhere mentioned. In fact, neither Ashvaghosha nor Bhāsa give any importance to Mahārāṣṭrī and it is Kalidasa who first introduces it in verses of his dramas and then, it becomes a common practice among the dramatists.

Back to Ashvaghosha. It is interesting that following the conventions and the injunctions of the Nāṭyaśāstra Ashvaghosha makes Gautama Buddha, the supreme *dhīrodātta* hero of his play *Shāriputra-prakaraṇa* speak in Sanskrit and not in Prakrit, although Buddha might never have spoken Sanskrit but would have preached all along in the so called Māgadhī Prakrit of his time which later came to be known as Pali. But Buddha was born as a prince and was educated too, so according to the literary convention, the author has let him speak Sanskrit.

Besides Buddha, the two Brahmins the noble and calm Shāriputra whom he converts and around whose conversion the plot is interwoven, his friend Maudgalāyana, the saintly Kauṇḍinya and the Shramaṇa speak Sanskrit whereas Prakrit is spoken by the ladies and the Vidūṣaka. In the fragments of the other two dramas of Ashvaghosha (of which one is allegorical similar to the Prabodhachandrodaya of Krishna Mishra and the other a play with a courtesan as the main heroine) there is a character called just 'Duṣṭa' who speaks Prakrit of 'Ardha-Māgadhī' variety of the grammarians which is very akin to Māgadhī since he replaces all 'r' with 'l', changes all sibilants into 'sh' and the nom. Sing. Mas. form ends on 'e' instead of an 'o'. Śaurasenī and Māgadhī are the other Prakrits used by him, the former by the Vidūṣaka and the courtesan and the latter by another character called 'Gobam'. The Śaurasenī of Ashvaghosha differs a little from its description in the later grammarians because it does not strictly change the intervocalic hard letters into soft, e.g. *bhavati* remains '*bhoti*' and does not become '*bhodi*'. The later developments are *hodi* and even *hoi*. Otherwise also the Śaurasenī of Ashvaghosha does not follow the grammatical rules as given by grammarians.

Ashvaghosa's Prakrit is much nearer to the Prakrit of Ashokan inscriptions, especially his Ardhamāgadhī. This court speech of Ashoka is believed to be a descendent of the Ardhamāgadhī of the last Tirthankar Mahavira (wrongly termed as Māgadhī in the sacred texts) which had assumed a quasi literary form during the time of Ashvaghosha. The Nāṭyaśāstra assigns the use of Ardhamāgadhī to scholars, sons of kings and rich merchants (i.e. the upper three *varṇas*) but its later use is much restricted and it appears only in the *Karṇabhāram* of Bhāsa.

Bhāsa is credited to have composed thirteen plays and a few might have been lost since the anthologies as well as some texts on Kāvyaśāstra quote quite a few verses under his names which are not found in his plays. But it could also be due to the fact that these plays—found only in Kerala – might be the abridged versions of the original plays done for the sake of their Keralite way of slow-motion presentation, as some scholars believe. His Prakrit exhibits a transitional phase between the Prakrits of Ashvaghosha and Kalidasa. It has no Mahārāṣṭrī verses in any of its dramas which are all composed in the Śaurasenī. Besides Śaurasenī, Bhāsa uses Māgadhī and occasionally also a little Ardhamāgadhī. The rule of grammarian to change the unvoiced intervocalic first and second letters to the third and fourth respectively in Śaursenī is not followed except in case of t and ṭ which are changed into d and ḍ respectively. For Sanskrit 'jñ' Ashvaghosh had 'ññ' in his Śaurasenī which is found in Pali texts as well. Later it regularly becomes ṇṇ (e.g. *paṇṇatti* for *prajñapti*) Bhāsa has it sometimes as ñ and at some other times as ṇ. He wavers between these two.

When we reach Kalidasa we are in the domain of regular Prakrit. He uses Śaurasenī for the prose dialogues and Mahārāṣṭrī for the beautiful verses incorporated in the dramas. The Mahārāṣṭrī seems to have become by his time the language of poetry due to the existence of such works as the *Gāthā Saptaśatī* of Haal. However Pischel in his *Prakrit Grammatick* has tried to show that the Mahārāṣṭrī verses of Kalidasa still betray some influence of Śaurasenī. The third language which he uses is Māgadhī which is spoken by the fisherman and the two police officers in the Shākuntalam. However, their higher officer does not speak Shakārī, also not Māgadhī, but the normal Śaurasenī. Some couplets in the *Vikramorvaśīyam* containing lamentation of Purūravā for Urvaśī, show traces of much later Prakrit, however, which comes rather nearer to its final phase which is known as Apabhraṃśa. These are mostly part of the Dhruvāgāna which is not always composed by the author of the play but usually by the stage director on ad *hoc* basis but when included in the manuscript, often becomes an integral part of the text.

The El Dorado of the Prakrit lovers is, however, the play *Mṛcchakaṭikam* in which seven different types of Prakrits are used – a few of which are not full-fledged Prakrit, but regional variations of not very great significance, although the Nāṭyaśāstra gives them full importance and call them vibhāṣās (dialects). These are Shakāri, Chaṇḍāli and Ṭakkī or Ḍhakkī.

Besides these three dialects the main Prakrits which are used are: Śaurasenī, Māgadhī, Prācyā and Avantikā. Mahārāṣṭrī, the most refined Prakrit and the language of Prakrit poetry has not been given its due and even the verses are in Śaurasenī. According to Prithvīdhara – the celebrated commentator on Mṛcchakaṭika — all the seven lady characters as well as four male characters speak Śaurasenī, Vidūṣaka speaks Prāchyā; six male characters including those belonging to the servant class as well as the son of Chārudatta speak Māgadhī and the two police officers of Ujjayini speak Avantikā, of these one speaks it with a southern accent. Shakāra has his own dialect called Shakārī which is a corrupt form of Māgadhī; the gamblers speak Ṭakkī. The stage director speaks both Sanskrit and Prakrit as per requirement. It appears that during the time when Mṛcchakaṭika was composed and was staged, these Prakrit varieties including their dialectical versions were living languages which could be accepted in the plays, since the audience not only comprehended them but could also identity them with different regions and with the clichés of the characteristics of the residents of those regions.

The main Prakrits of the Mṛcchakaṭika are also the living languages of the common parlance, the languages as they were really spoken. They have not been constructed as per rules of the Prakrit grammarians. The date of Mṛcchakaṭika must therefore not be too far away in time from the period when these Prakrits were living languages which I think points towards 1st to 3rd c. A.D.

As we proceed in time further and go beyond fifth century, the use of Prakrit gets limited mainly to two languages: Śaurasenī for the prose dialogues, interspersed occasionally by Māgadhī, and the use of Mahārāṣṭrī for the verses. *Mudrārākṣasa* and *Veṇīsaṃhāra* show this feature, so also the chaste Prakrit of the three dramas of Harsha which meticulously follow the rules laid down by Vararuchi or such other Prakrit grammarians. However by 800 or so, we observe that Bhavabhūti loses feeling for Prakrit, he seems to construct his Prakrit sentences in Sanskrit and converts them into Prakrit by applying the grammatical rules, especially of the phonetics. But it is noteworthy that inspite of this, the Prakrit of all these later dramas is not uniform because the Śaurasenī and Mahārāṣṭrī both admit a number of alternative forms due to their internal dialectical variations and the poets pick one of those as per their choice.

Although many of these Sanskrit plays written during the first millennium of Christian era use a very stylised and polished form of literary Prakrit which may not be akin to its spoken form of the age in which they were produced, yet it is not so well known that many of these so called "Sanskrit Nāṭakas" have the major part of their text going upto an extent of almost sixty per cent in Prakrit language, and much more so in the plays of the variety of *Nāṭikās* and *Saṭṭakas* which abound in female characters.

Strangely enough at a point of time when Prakrit must have ceased to be a spoken language and had made way for the early phase of New Indo-Aryan languages, which is around the tenth century, the Prakrit suddenly gets rejuvenated, perhaps due to the incessant efforts of the Jain munis and scholars who made it popular by their works composed entirely in Prakrit and this happens not only in North but also in South and mainly there. A new form of drama appears which is called *saṭṭaka* and is composed entirely in Prakrit. It consists mainly of female characters and is basically a dance drama. The word *saṭṭaka* is perhaps derived from Saaṭṭm where the Tamil-Malayalam word '*aṭṭm*' means dance, so *sa-aṭṭa* could be "with dance" or 'full of dance'. The "Karpūramañjarī" of Rajashekhara who hailed from Maharashtra-Karnatak region, and lived in the court of Kannauj in the tenth century is the first and the best *saṭṭaka* of its kind. Rajashekhara was very fond of Prakrit and has observed in this play that Prakrit is much more delicate and sweet than Sanskrit and that the difference between Sanskrit and Prakrit is akin to the difference between a man and a woman.

परुसा सक्कअबन्धा पाउअबन्धोवि होउ सुउमारो।
पुरुसमहिलाणं जेत्तिअ मिहन्तरं तेत्ति अमिमाणं।।

In imitation to Karpūramañjari or at least inspired by it, further *Saṭṭakas* were written among which *Rambhāmañjari* of Nayachandra (14th c.), *Vilāsavatī* by Mārkaṇḍeya (14th or 17th c.?), *Candalehā* by Rudradāsa (1660 AD), *Ānandasundarī* by Ghanashyāma (1730 AD) and *Singāramañjarī* by Vishveshwara (ca. 1750) are notable.

Function and Role of Prakrit:

Speaking about the rationale of the inclusion of Prakrit in Sanskrit plays the very first thing that one should bear in mind is the fact that the dramatic texts which we today call the "Sanskrit dramas" never refer to themselves as such. No author of these dramas has ever mentioned anywhere that he is going to write or has composed a "*Sanskrit drama*" (*rūpaka* or *nāṭaka*). The expression 'Sanskrit drama' is a modern term, whereas to every dramatist who composed these plays, it was clear and obvious from the very beginning, that the play has to be in the mixed languages of Sanskrit and Prakrit. The Nāṭyaśāstra nowhere uses the expression like '*Sanskrit-nāṭakāni*' or '*Sanskrit-rupakāṇi*'. On the contrary it recommends that the play has to be in the mixed form of languages which are spoken (or supposed to have been spoken) by the characters of the play *in real life* because a drama is a re-production or re-creation of a given event or situation (*avasthā-anukriti*) or '*bhāvānukīrtana*'. Further, for the sake of reality the male roles are to be performed by the males and the female roles by the females only; the female roles were never allowed to be performed by young boys dressed as females whereas this was regularly the case in the Greek drama or even in the Shakespearian theatre of the sixteenth century England.

And if females are doing the roles of female character, only their own innate language would look natural in their mouth which was Prakrit at the point when the Indian drama received its fully developed form. Speaking of Sanskrit by the ladies, except by those belonging to the educated elite class, would not only sound unnatural but would go against the theory of a 'true representation' of the situation; which the drama is supposed to be. It is the demand of the Reality since the drama has to be as real and as lifelike as it could be. It may further be added that for a person who is accustomed to speak Prakrit since his or her birth, an entirely refined and absolutely correct pronunciation of Sanskrit words, satisfying in every respect the learned audience, was certainly a difficult task to achieve. A humorous remark by the jester of Mṛcchakaṭika (Act III, vs. 3-4) is interesting in this context which says that a man becomes ridiculous trying to sing a Kākli which requires very high musical notes and a woman when she tries to speak Sanskrit because she renders all sibilants into *sa*, so that a lot of su-su sound is heard like the sound of breath exhaled by a cow when her nose has been pierced recently for putting a cord across.'

The second most important function of Prakrit in Sanskrit plays is its indispensability for providing the highly desirable musical atmosphere in the play. It is very often not realised how great a part the music plays in a successful and impressive dramatic performance.

Had it not been that important, the *Nāṭyaśāstra* would not have devoted seven full chapters dealing with the various aspects of music in drama. Not only a full fledged orchestra (*Kutapa*) is an indispensible part of drama, highlighting and strengthening the sentiments currently being depicted on stage, but the vocal part is also equally important, whether it comes from the *Nepathya* or is produced on stage. Most of the drama, one may remember, start with a song in Prakrit by the Naṭī at the request of the stage director. And then come the so called Dhruvā-s in-between again and again which are all and invariably in Prakrit. They are mostly not part of the written text but are composed, in Prakrit of course, by the stage director etc. and are introduced in the play from time to time. A song and its melody is enjoyed by the audience in a language that is used by them in daily practice. Only songs in our mother tongue are near and dear to our heart. We do not enjoy a song to that degree in a foreign language even though we may understand its meaning.

It would take us too far to talk about the various forms and functions of the Dhruvās, but we can at least note the following. In a Sanskrit drama the stage directions are at the barest minimum. The spectator makes out the situation, state of feeling, nature of the character, his occasion of appearance etc. from the sidelights and significant references in the speeches and dialogues that follows. Whatever is not expressly stated by the dramatist and has to be supplemented, is to be done by the songs which are called Dhruvās. There are five kinds of Dhruvās of which two are the Dhruvās of 'entrance' and 'exit' (*Prāveśikī/Naiṣkrāmikī*). The first introduces an important character to come on the stage, the second announces the departure of the character in the middle or at the end of an act. In between there are other dhruvās – *Prāsādiki, Ākṣepikī* and *Antarā*. Prāsādikī reinforces a mood or situation, Akṣepikī announces some event which is not shown on the stage but is important to understand the further course of action and the last, the Antarā is sung when a gap or mishap in the production has to be covered up or when due to an overpowering feeling of grief, or madness of love, loss of memory, sleep etc., there is a tense pause in the action of the play. The best example of this variety are the Dhruvās which are found in the fourth act of the *Vikramorvashīyam* and which are composed in a kind of very late Prakrit, as mentioned above, which seems to approach almost the level of Apabhraṃsha of, say, the 8th-9th century. These contain out-pourings of a love-lorn and desolate Puruvravā at the disappearance of his love, the divine damsel Urvashī.

The language of these Dhruvās has baffled a number of critics. How could Kalidasa compose these songs in a such a late variety of Prakrit, is the question which finds its perfect solution and answer that these Dhruvās were not all written by the poet himself but introduced by the producers of the play taking the lead of the verses and statements appearing in the play as well as the situation prevailing. They were later added to the script of the play and became gradually part of the text.

The other very important function of the Prakrit is to present of the audience an analysis of the situation from the point of view of the common men. A Sanskrit play is usually written from the elitist point of view and depicts the activities taking place in the higher strata of the society, mostly in royal palaces.

How the activities of these higher ups are viewed by the common man is usually depicted by the character of Vidūṣaka through his plain and satirical remarks which find easy access to the hearts of the common audience and win the support of the viewers for his views. The criticism of the Vidūṣaka who is very close to the hero of the play – yet a common man, sees the things in a very practical manner from the perspective of the common public as it would generally see and understand it.

I cite an example from the *Abhijñāna Shākuntalam* of Kalidasa. As is known, the activity of hunting was one of the most favourite pastimes of the kings of all the times. It has also been glorified by the poets. A king occasionally leaves with his retinue of hunters and army chiefs etc. to a forest where a temporary shelter is erected for him. It is all right for him to live in a camp where he is properly looked after by a host of his servants but it causes a lot of inconvenience and suffering to the members of his crew. The point of view of these persons is beautifully described by Kalidasa through Vidūṣaka in the AS. The whole passage is a soliloquy of him on the stage in the Prakrit language:

> "Oh my dammned fate: I am really disgusted with my friendship with this king who is so possessed of the hunting! 'Here is a deer' 'There is a boar' 'Yonder is a tiger' thus at this midday of summer we wander about from forest to forest amid rows of woods which hardly have shades due to getting thinned in summer. We drink hot, stinking waters of mountain-torrents, astringent from the mixture of dry leaves fallen in them. Indefinitely and at very irregular hours, we get our meal consisting chiefly of grilled meet roasted on spikes. Even in the night I cannot sleep because all my joints are aching due to running after the horses. Then, even before it is dawn, these bastard ("sons of slave girls") fowl hunters let loose their fiercely barking dogs against the birds and also wake me up for accompanying them. But as if this misery were not enough, a boil has grown on my tumour. Another misfortune has befallen me. Due to my ill fate, yesterday while we were all away, this our master entered the penance grove of Kaṇva where he chanced upon a certain hermit's daughter and look, he is now not at all talking or thinking of going back to the capital. . . .!"

The author further suggests that everyone is weary of this long stay in the forest but is afraid to say so to the king. On the suggestion of the Vidūṣaka to wind up the whole operation, the king calls Senāpati who is happy to learn that the king is seriously considering to stop hunting. He says aside to the Vidūṣaka "well done! You continue to be firm on what you say, but let me say to the king what he *wants* to hear from me!" And then to the king he says "Oh, this foolish Brahmin is talking non-sense. Hunting is the most wonderful and entertaining pastime which shapes up the body. Which else is such an interesting and healthy sport?!" He then goes on citing the advantages of the activity. The hypocrisy and flattery of the courtiers is thus brought to light. The Senāpati, an officer of high rank speaking Sanskrit is not allowed to speak before the king what he thinks right. The Prakrit speaking Vidūṣaka does not have to consider that, he is free to say what he thinks right and presents the counter perspective.

Another great contribution of the Prakrit to the Sanskrit drama is to lighten the serious atmosphere of the play with humour. Humour can be created only in the language of common parlance – in the living language of common people. We enjoy humour and jokes mainly in our own colloquial language. Jokes are created through the incongruities, whether real or imaginative, of our daily life and experience. Sanskrit dramas like '*Hāsyārṇava*' and '*Hāsyachūḍāmaṇi*' fail to evoke humour in us because they are about a society and a milieu which is not ours, and are in a language which is not our daily tongue. Mṛcchakaṭika has many passages in Prakrit evoking hilarious laughter among the common audience, not only through the absurd mythological references of the stupid, arrogant and ignorant Śakāra when he refers to Kuntī as being kidnapped by Rāvaṇa (I. 21) or to the abduction of Subhadrā, the sister of Vishvāvasu as per his knowledge by Hanumān, but also through the capacity of Prakrit language to have more than one meaning of a particular word, because very often two or more Sanskrit word coalesce and have only one and the same form in Prakrit.

The variety of this sort of humour created by the Prakrit words allowing double meaning is amply found in the Mṛīcchakaṭika, especially in its fifth act in the dialogues between the Vidūṣaka Vasantaka and Kumbhīlaka, the servant of Vasantasenā, who comes to Charudatta's place to announce the visit of Vasantasenā. In the course of their conversation, Kumbhīlaka once says to Vasantaka: "*ale paṇham te daissam*" upon which the latter retorts: "*ahaṃ te muṇḍe goḍam daissam.*" The servant means to say that he wants to put a question (*praśna*) to the Vidūṣaka but the word *paṇham* is very near to the word *paṇhi* which means the foot-sole (*pārṣṇi*) and also *paṇa* – a small coin. The Vidūṣaka deliberately hears and interprets it in a different way and his answer apparently means: 'I shall give you a kick *goḍa* (meaning leg, even to this day) on your head' but this word is also near to *gaṇḍa* which means a higher coin containing four *paṇas*. So the sense as comprehended by the public is: If the servant were to hit Vidūṣaka with the sole of his foot, the Vidūshaka thereupon shall give him a kick on the head, or if the servant gives a *paṇas* to Vidūṣaka, he gets in return four times more, a *gaṇḍa* from him. Further the instruction of Kumbhīlaka to utter the words (*padam*) *senā* and *vasanta* by reversing their order (*padāiṃ palivattāvehi*), the Vidūṣaka understands the expression as '*pādān parivartya*' (reversing the legs) and assumes a cross-legged position before speaking the words in the very same order (Senāvasante). Such humours and witty puns are possible only when the dramatist uses the Prakrit expressions. And when we render such passages in Sanskrit for students, the pun gets lost and the sense becomes unintelligible. Sanskrit does not come down to this level of local parlance which could create small but witty humour on commonplace subjects.

I feel that it is the Prakrit in the Sanskrit dramas which has made it lively and lifelike, otherwise it would not have served it's avowed purpose mentioned in the NS of "*lokānurañjana*" i.e. the entertainment of common masses and for giving peace and solace to the poor souls (*tapasvin*) who are exhausted after toiling the whole day (*śramārta*), who are afflicted with grief (*śokārta*), are distressed and desperate (*duḥkhārta*); and instead of all that, it would have attained more or less the character either of a high piece of literature fit only for reading - that too try scholars, or more or less the character of a ritual text which in its very inception it perhaps was.

3

Adhivedana – The Ancient Indian Practice of Divorce

Radhavallabh Tripathi

It is a common belief that marriage according to Hindu scriptures is irrevocable being a sacrament and a divinely ordained relationship. The very concept of a wife as the half of her husband spelled out in most unequivocal terms[1] in Vedic literature overrules any idea of any kind of separation in marriage.

The *mantras* recited during the ritual for solemnizing a marriage make the bridegroom to promise a union with his would–be wife till old-age.[2] He would also declare that the bond of marriage would remain intact till the last moment of his life.[3] The blessings given by the elders, which form a part of the ritual, repeatedly say that the couple should remain ever united.[4]

---

[1]अर्ध जाया मनुष्यस्य। अर्धो ह एष आत्मनो यज्जायेति। *Śatapaṭhabrāhmaṇa*, V.2.1.10

यावन्न विन्दते जायो तावदर्धो भवेत् पुमान्।

नार्ध प्रजायते सर्व प्रजायेतेत्यपि श्रुतिः।। *Vyāsasmṛti* -14, *Aṣṭādaśasmṛti*, p. 424

[2] गृभ्णामि ते सौभगत्वाय हस्तं मया पत्या जरदष्टिर्यथासः। *Ṛgveda*, X.85.25

[3] प्रेतो मुञ्चामि नामुतः सुबद्धामुतस्करम्। *Ṛgveda*, X.85.25

[4] इहैव स्तं मा वियोष्टं विश्वमायुर्व्यश्नुतम्। *Atharvaveda*, X.85.25

अग्निः सुभगां जातवेदा पत्ये पत्नीं जरदष्टिर्यथासः। *ibid*, XIV.1.49

The authors of *Dharmasūtras* like *Āpastambha* treat the bond of marriage absolutely irrevocable, the violation of which would cause both of the defaulters to fall in hell;[5] *Āpastambha* also prescribes an exceptionally harsh punishment for a man deserting his wife – "wearing donkey's skin, he should beg for feeding himself from seven houses making an announcement – 'please give alms for a man who has wronged his wife!'. He should live this way for six months."[6] The lady making the similar kind of violation is required to observe the *kṛcchravrata* for twelve nights.[7]

There are different views in the *smṛtis* on the questions whether a woman proven to have had illicit relations with a man should be deserted by her husband or not. To some of the authors of *dharmasūtras*, neither the adultery committed by a wife, nor any act unbecoming of the matrimonial relationship can be considered the reason for the breach of the relationship.[8]

Adultery is of two types mild and aggressive, and the authors of *dharmaśāstra* texts do not favor divorce even for a woman who is an aggressive adulteress – *ugra vyabhicāriṇī*. Punishments to a wife betraying her husband are provided for, but in no case she is to be deserted or divorced. A woman is never impure, she is purified after every menstruation.[9]

On the other hand, *Vyabhicāra* (adultery) by a woman is a condemnable offence for other *smṛtikāras*, a woman indulging in *vyabhicāra* is to be renounced with minimum allowance for her maintenance.[10]

---

5 तद्व्यतिक्रमे पुनरुभयोर्नरकः। *Āpastambhadharmasūtra*, II.10.27.6

6 दारव्यतिक्रमी खराजिनं बहिर्लोम परिधाय दारव्यतिक्रमिणे भिक्षामिति सप्तागाराणी चरेत्। सा वृत्तिः षण्मासान्। *ibid*, I.10.28.19

7 स्त्रियास्तु भर्तुर्व्यतिक्रमे कृच्छ्रद्वादशरात्राभ्यासस्ताबन्तं कालम्। *ibid*, I.10.28.20

व्यतिक्रमे तु कृच्छ्रः, शूद्रे चान्द्रायणं चरेत्। *Bodhāyanadharmasūtra*, II.2.3.49-50

8 न त्याज्या दुष्कृता नारी नास्यास्त्यागो विधीयते।

मासि मासि रजो ह्यासां दुष्कृतान्यपकर्षति। *Vaśiṣṭhadharmasūtra*, XXVIII.3-4

9 *Atrisaṃhitā*, 190-96, *Aṣṭādaśasmṛti*, pp. 30-31

10 हृताधिकारां मलिनां पिण्डमात्रोपजीविनीम्।

परिभूतामधःशय्यां वासयेद् व्यभिचारिणीम्॥ *Yājñyavalkyasmṛti*, I.70

Forsaking a married woman, who has not done anything wrong, is regarded highly sinful.[11]

Professor P. Ramchandrudu has been a well-known Sanskrit scholar steeped in tradition and open to modern notions. He has authored a new *dharmaśāstra* text in Sanskrit – *Kauṇḍinyasmṛti.* Despite his progressive outlook on several areas, he condemns the modern practice of divorce in this *smṛti* – "The bond of marriage between man and woman is unbreakable. Marriage is a source of mutual happiness of man and woman both here and hereafter. The woman and man are the two wheels of the cart of the worldly life. There is no difference in their strength or in place of honour of both of them; this is *sanātana dharma.* No woman can live without man and no man can live without woman. The talk of antagonism heard now and then, should be treated as *praṇayakopa,* feigned anger in love. The break of marriage again and again on flimsy grounds would be cause of ruin of the family and unrest in society. Children born out of marriage lasting only for two or three or five or six years would become highly undisciplined without any control. Those who cut the bond of marital relation on account of lust, bad temper or haughtiness or fickle-mindedness will have to undergo series of troubles in the old age." (tr. by Ramachandrudu himself).[12]

---

11 अदृष्टापचितां भार्यां यौवने परित्यजेत्।
सप्त जन्म भवेत् तस्य स्त्रीत्वं वैधव्यं च पुनः:पुनः॥ *Parāśarasmṛti*-15, *Aṣṭādaśasmṛti*, p. 243

12 स्त्रीपुंसयोरविच्छेद्यः बन्धो वैवाहिको मतः।
अन्योन्यस्यातिमहते सुखायात्र परत्र च।।
संसारशकटस्योक्ते द्वे चक्रे स्त्री पुमानिति।
शक्तिर्मानस्तयोस्तुल्यावेष धर्मः सनातनः॥
न नरेण विना नारी न नार्या च विना नरः।
तदा तदा द्वेषभाषा ग्राह्या प्रणयकोपवत्॥
पुनः पुनर्विवाहस्य च्छेदः क्षुद्रेण हेतुना।
विनाशाय कुटुम्बस्य समाजस्याप्यशान्तये॥
द्वित्रपञ्चषवर्षात्मकालदाम्पत्ययोर्हि या।
सन्ततिः स्याद् दुर्विनीता समाजेऽशान्तिकारणम्॥
कामेन दुरहङ्कृत्या विवाहं चापलेन वा।
छिन्दतां वार्धकेऽनन्ता भवेत् क्लेशपरम्परा॥ *Kauṇḍinyasmṛti*, 183-88

There are instances of men forsaking their wives as described in the Epics and the *Purāṇas*, though they may not be taken as the cases of divorce exactly in the legal sense of the term as understood today. In *Rāmāyaṇa*, the King of Kaikeya made a declaration of divorcing his queen, whom he had legally married. King Daśaratha, outraged at Kaikeyī's demand of two boons, makes a declaration to forsake her. While in the first case, the declaration of the divorce was actually carried out by the King of Kaikaya, in the second case, it just remained confined to a wishful thinking of the king who met his demise soon after. In the *Rāmāyaṇa*, Rāma who has just defeated Rāvaṇa, speaks in utterly harsh tones to Sitā and refuses to admit her as his wife and even asks her to go to any man anywhere in the world. He does bring her to *Ayodhyā* after the fire-test, but finally banishes her to save the reputation of the great family of the *Raghus*. In the *Mahābhārata*, Duḥṣanta secretly marries Śakuntalā, and when she comes to demand her right as a wife, he deliberately refuses to recognize her with a roguish arrogance and pretentions. Ahalyā in Rāmāyaṇa is an example of a forsaken woman. There are stories of women, like Damayantī or Yaśodharā, who were forsaken by their husbands without any kind of intimation or explanation. In the *nāyikābheda* (categories of heroines), the *vipralabdhā* almost approximates a divorcee.

In the *Mahābhārata* Pāṇdu tells Kunti that women in former ages were uncontrollable, they did as they liked and left one man for the other. This promiscuity belonged a bygone age. Even then there are instances of ladies leaving their husbands at their will. The women of Therīgātghā, leave their house and the husband to join the *saṅgha.* But these acts of renunciation also can not be taken as the cases of divorce in the legal sense of the term as understood today.

A house-holder would not be allowed to become an ascetic without the permission of his wife, which overruled any license to a man for forsaking a duly married wife. But this also implies that he may divorce his wife if she permits him to do so. There are instances of wives permitting their husbands for *sannyāsa*, and the husbands willfully availing this opportunity. At least two of the disciples of Śaṅkarācārya – Umveka and Padmapāda – did so.

The question then remains – did the *dharmaśāstras* permit divorce? The pundits in our times take considerable pride in emphasizing over the unbreakable nature of matrimonial relationship in Hindu society. On the other hand, the scholars with a modern outlook are not comfortable with this and some of them find this enforced permanency in marriage as inhuman and unjustified. One of them has pathetically complained that Sanskrit language does not even contain a word for divorce.[13]

Both of these – the puritans and the protestants – either disregard or are unaware of, the whole gamut of terms which *smṛtis* use to spell out the idea of separation and divorce between married people. These terms include *mokṣa* (being free from each other), *adhivedana* (partial divorce), *tyāga* and *parityāga* (renouncement), *nirvāsana* (banishment) *niṣkrāmaṇa* (expulsion), *nirdamana* (eviction or deportation) etc. which approximate the idea of divorce between married people with considerable difference. The way Manu prohibits *mokṣa* in matrimony gives sufficient ground for the belief that in actual practice the couple did separate and got divorced.

The term *mokṣa* is used by Kauṭilya in the sense of complete divorce between a husband and a wife, with specific legal provisions. While Kauṭilya allows a woman to form sexual relations with other man, preferably the younger brother of her own husband, in case the husband is away from home for a long time. He also gives the liberty tc a woman for divorcing the husband if he has committed something disgraceful, has gone on a prolonged journey, has revolted against the state, or if he is a criminal or is impotent.[14] He also allows divorce on mutual consent to the couple if their marriages were not solemnized by vedic rites. A man is allowed to seek divorce from the woman doing a disservice to him.[15] But then Kauṭilya also adds that

---

[13] सच बात यह है कि संस्कृत भाषा में तलाक के अर्थ का कोई शब्द नहीं है। यदि संस्कृत भाषा में तलाक के लिये शब्द होता, तो बुद्ध को घर छोड़ कर भागना न पड़ता।

संस्कृत भाषा में तलाक और डाइवोर्स के अर्थ का शब्द नदारद है। *Kāmasūtra kī Santānen: Dharmavir,* p. 15

[14] नीचत्वं परदेशं वा प्रस्थितो राजकिल्बिषी।

प्राणाभिहन्ता पतितस्त्याज्यः क्लीबोऽपि वा पतिः॥ *Arthaśāstra*, part II, p. 18

[15] Ibid, part II, p. 21

mokṣa is not to be given in case of marriages sanctified by vedic rites (*dharmya-vivāhas*).[16]

Devala in his *smṛti* seems to have used the word *mokṣa* in the sense of divorce in context of property to be inherited by a woman. Nīlakaṇṭha has interpreted it as *tyāga* which means *dāna* (charity). But looking to the context, I think that Devala has used the term *mokṣa* to mean divorce here.[17]

Adhidevana involves various steps getting separated from the wife considering the nature of the offense committed by her, i.e. stopping conversation, termination of conjugal relationships, prohibition from rituals, arranging a different dwelling or sending her to her kin. Manu has extensively dealt with the renouncement of a wife who is rude, hateful or exhibits bad character. He has used the terms *tyāga*, *parityāga* and *adhivedana* synonymously in this context.

The word *mokṣa* in Sanskrit comes from the root *mokṣa*, basically meaning to release, to be released. The state of being released is *mokṣa*. *Mukti*, its synonym is formed by the root *muc* meaning to renounce, which Manu has used with prefix *vi* The way Manu prohibits vimukti or *mokṣa* in matrimony gives sufficient ground for the belief that in actual practice the couple did separate and got divorced. "*Vimocana* of a wife from the husband is possible neither by sale nor by desertion" – he says – "we know this as *dharma* which the Prajāpati prescribed."[18]

But then there are passages in Manu opening the possibilities of a wife remarrying and a husband obtaining a legal separation from his wife for a limited period. The two stanzas in IX.76 states that a woman should wait for her husband for eight years in case he has

---

16 अमोक्षो धर्म्यविवाहानाम्। *Arthaśāstra*, part II, p. 18

17 वृत्तिराभरणं शुल्कं लाभश्च स्त्रीधनं भवेत्।
भोक्त्री च स्वयमेवेदं पतिर्नार्हत्यानापदि।
वृथा (तथा ?) मोक्षे च भोगे च स्त्रियै दद्यात् सवृद्धिकम्।
पुत्रार्तिहरणे वाऽपि स्त्रीधनं भोक्तुमर्हति॥
मोक्षस्त्यागो दानमिति यावत्। *Vyavahāramayūkha of Nīlakaṇṭha*, p. 100. Suggested reading in bracket is mine.

18 न निष्क्रयविसर्गाभ्यां भर्तुर्भार्या विमुच्यते। एवं धर्मं विजानीमः प्राक्प्रजापतिनिर्मितम्॥ *Manusmṛti*, IX.46

proceeded on a long journey for an act of *dharma*, for six years if he has proceeded for studies or fame and for three years if he has gone for pleasure.[19] This has led the commentators to make a number of suggestions as to what she should do after the expiry of the term of waiting – taking another husband being one of them. Kulūkabhaṭṭa's suggestion seems to be most practicable – that the lady should go to live with her husband. But Kulūka does not consider the situation as to what the woman should do if she does not know his whereabouts, is unable to locate him, and is turned out even if she finds him.

But then, Manu makes a clear provision for stopping *samvāsa* (living together) with a woman who hates her husband after waiting just for one year. After a year the husband should take away her inheritance and stop relationships with her—he says.[20] Kulūkabhṭta suggests that she should be provided with bare minimum subsistence –(*grāsamātrācchchādanaṃ tu deyam eva*).

The instruction does not imply banishment from the house. In the next stanza there is a provision for forsaking a wife for three months allowing her to take her ornaments and other things.[21] Brian Smith's translation – 'He may deprive her of jewellery and personal property' does not fit in the context as in the very next stanza Manu prohibits complete desertion even of a hateful woman and he also prohibits depriving her of her property.[22]

Adhivinnā is translated as supersession, deprivation conjugal rights, forsaking a wife and taking another., *i.e.* a lady, subjected to this partial divorce is to live separately with provision of maintenance. It involves gradations for disserting and depriving the woman of the status of a housewife, but it cannot normally include expulsion. Manu

---

19 प्रोषितो धर्मकार्यार्थं प्रतीक्ष्योऽष्टौ नरः समाः ।
विद्यार्थं षड्यशोऽर्थं वा कामार्थं त्रींस्तु वत्सरान् ॥ *Manusmṛti*, IX.76

20 संवत्सरं प्रतीक्षेत द्विषन्तीं योषितं पतिः ।
ऊर्ध्वं संवत्सरात्त्वेनां दायं हृत्वा न संवसेत् ॥ Ibid, IX.77

21 अतिक्रामेत्प्रमत्तं या मत्तं रोगार्तं एव वा ।
सा त्रीन्मासान्परित्याज्या विभूषणपरिच्छदा ॥ Ibid, IX.78

22 उन्मत्तं पतितं क्लीबं अबीजं पापरोगिणम् ।
न त्यागोऽस्ति द्विषन्त्याश्च न च दायापवर्तनम् ॥ Ibid, IX.79

also prescribes absolute *adhivedana*, which amount to complete desertion of a woman, if she is a drunkard, is of a loose character, goes against the man, suffers from (an incurable) disease, has violent and murderous designs.[23] Yājñavalkya says that a woman who has betrayed her husband should be shorn of all the rights (of a wife), is made live unclean and on minimum subsistence, in humiliating conditions and has to sleep on a separate and lower bed. Yajñavalkya also prescribes *Adhivedana* for the woman who is a drunkard, inflicted with some disease, is a rogue, is barren, wastes money, speaks unpleasant words, gives birth to female children only and is envious to the man.[24] Manu has used the terms *tyāga*, *parityāga* and *adhivedana* synonymously in this context. But a woman subjected to *tyāga*, *parityāga* and *adhivedana* is not be banished from the husband's house.

There prescribed limits to allow the wife under *adhivedana* the time for reforming herself. They range between eight to eleven years, whereas there is provision of instant divorce for a woman who speaks harsh words.[25]

Manu makes all sorts of concessions for a man desirous forsaking his wife. He is somewhat kind to the lady of good conduct and prescribes that a woman who is either ill or is kind-hearted and imbued with good character should only be given *adhivedana* after getting her consent and even after being given *adhivedana* she should never be humiliated.[26] Expelling a wife who has been given *adhivedana* is prohibited in Manu. If such a woman leaves the house in fury she should be stopped (Brian translated 'locked up')

---

[23] मद्यपासाधुवृत्ता च प्रतिकूला च या भवेत्।
व्याधिता वाधिवेत्तव्या हिंस्रार्थघ्नी च सर्वदा॥ Ibid, IX.80

[24] हृताधिकारां मलिनां पिण्डमात्रोपजीविनीम्।
परिभूतामधःशय्यां वासयेद् व्यभिचारिणीम्॥
सुरापी व्याधिता धूर्ता वन्ध्यार्थघ्न्यप्रियंवदा।
स्त्रीप्रसूश्चाधिवेत्तव्या पुरुषद्वेषिणी तथा॥ *Yājñavalkyasmṛti*, I.70,72

[25] वन्ध्याष्टमेऽधिवेद्याऽब्दे दशमे तु मृतप्रजा।
एकादशे स्त्रीजननी सद्यस्त्वप्रियवादिनी॥ Ibid, IX.81

[26] या रोगिणी स्यात्तु हिता संपन्ना चैव शीलतः।
सानुज्ञाप्याधिवेत्तव्या नावमान्या च कर्हिचित्॥ Ibid, IX.82

or be dispatched to her parental house.[27] Kulūkabhaṭṭa says that she should be stopped by binding with ropes etc. till she calms down (*rajjvādinā baddhā sthāpanīyā ākopanivṛtteḥ*).[28] Yājñavalkya is also of the opinion that there is no need to go to the extant of *adhivedana* for an adulteress. But if she is pregnant (by another man) they she should be deserted. Vijñāneśvara adds here that *tyāga* has to be done in case of heinous crimes like pregnancy and murder of the husband (*garbhabhartṛvadhādau tathā mahati pātake*). But then an *adhivinnā* – the woman thus deserted should be provided maintenance, failing which the husband would incur great sin.

Commentators of Yajnavalkya prescribe *tyāga* has several gradations – stopping conversation, stopping conjugal relations, prohibiting the wife from participation in rituals, lodging her in another house. For all these categories of divorce, the he law-givers insist on providing maintenance for the ladies partially divorced, renounced or separated with difference in the grades of whether it is *mokṣa, adhivedana,* or *nirvāsana.* Yājñavalkya also says that the man has to continue supporting even a woman who has committed the most serious offences, otherwise he would incurs great sin[29] and on the other hand if he renounces a wife who is obedient, skilled, has produced brave sons, and is soft-spoken, then he should be made to provide one third of his earnings a maintenance for the lady. If he is penniless, then he is to take responsibility to support her.[30] Vijñāneśvara says that this is equally applicable to a man who marries another lady when he already has a good wife. Even if he is penniless, he has to take responsibility to support her.

---

[27] Brian has translated as 'deserted in presence of the family' But Kulūkabhaṭṭa's explanation to me is more authentic – *pitrādikulasannidhau vā tyājyā* i.e. she should be sent to her parental house.

[28] अधिविन्ना तु या नारी निर्गच्छेद्रुषिता गृहात्।
सा सद्यः संनिरोद्धव्या त्याज्या वा कुलसंनिधौ॥ Ibid, IX.83

[29] अधिविन्ना तु भर्तव्या महदेनोऽन्यथा भवेत्। *Yājñavalkyasmṛti*, I.74
त्वग्दुष्टां व्यसनासक्तां महितामधिवेदयेत्।
अधिविन्नामपि विभुः स्त्रीणां तु समतामियात्॥ *Vyāsasmṛti*, IX.81

[30] आज्ञासम्पादिनीं दक्षां वीरसूं प्रियवादिनीम्।
त्यजन् दाप्यस्तृतीयांशमद्रव्यो भरणं स्त्रियाः॥ *Yājñavalkyasmṛti*, I.76

The injunctions with regard to *punarbhū* (a lady married again) by the authors of *smṛti* texts indicate a silence acceptance of divorce. The *purnarbhū* is given a legal status with provisions for inheriting the property of the previous or the second husband. *Atharvaveda* describes the practice of a married lady renouncing one husband and choosing another.[31] Vātsyāyana in his *Kāmasūtra* (IV.2.35) recommends that a lady may leave her husband and go to live with another man if she does not feel amenability. (*ātmanaścittānukūlyāt iti Vātsyāyānaḥ* – Kāmasūtra, IV.2.35). Vātsyāyana also makes provisions to help this lady to enable her to lead an honourable and comfortable life. Parāśara prescribes re-marriage of a lady in five situations – the husband is lost, is dead, has become an ascetic, is impotent, is condemned.[32]

The concept that a woman is the field to be owned by the one who has the seed, allows room for getting her divorced from the man who has no seed. Jay Shankar Prasad in his well known Hindi play *Dhruvasvāminī*, a modern classic, had invoked a passage from Nārada airing this view and also the recommendation of Parāśara for remarrying a women in case of five calamities to justify the re-marriage of Dhruvasvāminī with Candragupta, who was the younger brother of her husband Rāmagupta. Prasad also projected her as a lady with revolutionary spirit.

The authors of the texts on *vyavahāra* (Law) belonging to the medieval period are aware of the ancient practice of women divorcing a man and re-marrying. Devaṇabhaṭṭa cites the views of Vaśiṣṭha prescribing re-marriage (punaḥ-saṁsāra) of a girl married with vedic rites, in case she has not been made to loose her virginity.[33]

---

[31] *Atharvaveda*, IX.5.27-28

[32] नष्टे मृते प्रव्रजिते क्लीबे च पतिते पतौ।
पञ्चस्वापत्सु नारीणां पतिरन्यो विधीयते॥ *Parāśarasmṛti* -31, *Aṣṭādaśasmṛti*, p. 345

[33] पाणिग्रहकृते कन्या केवलं मन्त्रसंस्कृता
सा चेदक्षतयोनिः स्यात् पुनः संस्कारमर्हति॥
उद्वाहितापि या कन्या न चेत् सम्प्राप्तमैथुना
पुनः संस्कारमर्हेत यथा कन्या तथैव सा॥ *Smṛticandrikā*, pp. 221-23

Most revolutionary verdict in this context is given by *Yamasmṛti* as cited by *Smṛticandrikā*, which says – If the husband is not suitable in family and character, then even if a girl is married by *mantras*, that does make a ground for getting her released from this unsuitable marriage. She should be taken out of the house of her in-laws by applying force and be married to a deserving man. This is the view of Śātātapa. Devaṇabhaṭṭa also cites Kātyāyana who holds almost the similar view,[34] and he also cites the view of Parāśara, prescribing re-marriage in five calamities, albeit ascribing it to Manu. But to Devaṇabhaṭṭa these are just prima facie views. He over rules them by simply saying these were in practice in the days of yore, but in Kaliyuga they are prohibited. There are alternate *smṛtis* for this age, which absolutely prohibit re-marriage.[35] He however, does supports desertion of the wife of unbecoming conduct.

Manu has listed eighteen *mārgas* (ways, categories) of *vyavahāras*[36] (law-suits) for a court of law (which is called *sabhā, dharmādhikaraṇa, dharmāsana* or *dharmasthāna* in different texts)[37]. These categories have been called *vivādapadas* (issues for dispute) by later authors and the list of Manu has been mostly reproduced by them. *Strīpuṁdharma*

---

34 वरश्च कुलशीलाभ्यां न युज्येत कथञ्चन
न मन्त्रः कारणं तत्र न च कन्यानृतं भवेत्।
समाकृष्य तु तां कन्यां बलादक्षतयोनिकाम्
पुनर्गुणवते दद्यादिति शातातपोब्रवीत्॥
कात्यायनोपि --
स तु स्यादन्यजातीयः पतितः क्लीब एव वा
ऊढापि देया साऽन्यस्मै सप्रावारणभूषणा॥ Ibid, p.224

35 ऊढाया पुनरुद्वाहं ज्येष्ठांशं गोवधं तथा।
कलौ पञ्च न कुर्वीत भ्रातृजायां कमण्डलुम्॥ Ibid, p.225

36 *Vyavahāra* has been defined by *Yājñavalkya* as a petition made before a king by a person who has been made to suffer by others in contravention to the codes of conduct prescribed in the smṛtis (स्मृत्याचारव्यपेतेन मार्गेणाधर्षितः परैः। आवेदयति चेद् राज्ञे व्यवहारपदं हि तत्॥ *Yājñavalkyasmṛti*, II.5)

37 Bṛhaspati has used the word *sabhā* for the law-court, Kātyāyana used a more appropriate title- *dharmādhikaraṇa*. (*Vyavahāramayūkha* of Nīlakaṇṭha, p. 6) Bhavabhūti has used the word *dharmāsana* in his *Uttararāmacaritam* for Rāma's court room.

(laws related to man and woman) is one of these *vivādapadas* in the list.[38]

It seems unlikely that a man or least of all a woman, would approach a *sabhā* or *dharmādhikaraṇa* for the request of *mokṣa* under the *vyavahāra* of *Strīpuṁdharma*, i.e. to file a suit for divorce. From Nīlakaṇṭha's description of *strīpuṃdharma* in *Vyavahāramayūkha* we understand that *strīpuṃdharma* is comprised of instructions to the king to see that the men do not renounce their wives and the wives should also not leave their husbands.[39] But again the authors of *Smṛtis* and specially the Purāṇa do leave a scope of a petition for divorce in the royal court of law. The *Agnipurāṇa* has also enumerated eighteen categories of disputes called *vivādapadas* (law-suits) in a *sabhā* (court of law). With regard to the *vivādapada* named *strīpuṃdharma*, it says - "A king's court shall entertain suits in which the legality of a marriage or the fulfillment of any condition appertaining thereto, is contested or sought to be enforced either by the husband or the wife, and such a suit shall be denominated as Marriage – suit".[40] (tr. in the ed. of Maitreyi Deshpande, Vol. II, p. 890)

---

[38] व्यवहारान्दिदृक्षुस्तु ब्राह्मणैः सह पार्थिवः।
मन्त्रज्ञैर्मन्त्रिभिश्चैव विनीतः प्रविशेत्सभाम्॥
तत्रासीनः स्थितो वापि पाणिमुद्यम्य दक्षिणम्।
विनीतवेषाभरणः पश्येत्कार्याणि कार्यिणाम्॥
प्रत्यहं देशदृष्टैश्च शास्त्रदृष्टैश्च हेतुभिः।
अष्टादशसु मार्गेषु निबद्धानि पृथक्पृथक्॥
तेषामाद्यं ऋणादानं निक्षेपोऽस्वामिविक्रयः।
संभूय च समुत्थानं दत्तस्यानपकर्म च॥
वेतनस्यैव चादानं संविदश्च व्यतिक्रमः।
क्रयविक्रयानुशयो विवादः स्वामिपालयोः॥
सीमाविवादधर्मश्च पारुष्ये दण्डवाचिके।
स्तेयं च साहसं चैव स्त्रीसंग्रहणं एव च॥
स्त्रीपुंधर्मो विभागश्च द्यूतमाह्वय एव च॥
पदान्यष्टादशैतानि व्यवहारस्थिताविह॥
एषु स्थानेषु भूयिष्ठं विवादं चरतां नृणाम्।
धर्मं शाश्वतं आश्रित्य कुर्यात्कार्यविनिर्णयम्॥ *Manusmṛti* VIII.1-8

[39] *Vyavahāramayūkha* of Nīlakaṇṭha, p. 159-60

[40] वैवाहिको विधिः स्त्रीणां पुंसां यत्र च कीर्त्यते।
स्त्रीपुंसयोगसंज्ञं तु तद् विवादपदं स्मृतम्॥ *Agnipurāṇa*, 253.24

Vijnāneśvara and Caṇḍeśvara say that the *vivādapada* called *strīpuṃdharma* is meant to keep the husband and the wife maintain their *dharma*. Vijnāneśavara cites the tradition upholding that family matters, specially disputes between the husband and the wife were not supposed to be brought under litigation.[41] But then he explains that this injunction cannot be absolute. Whenever there is a necessity, the disputes amongst these will also form law-suits.[42] He even says that if a king comes to know of some offence committed by the husband or the wife directly or indirectly, he should take suo-motto notice.[43]

The possibilities of seeking a divorce may arise mostly in families where women are allowed to make their own earning by doing a job. Manu provides for a lady's doing a job if the husband has proceeded on a long journey and has not arranged for her 'livelihood by crafts that are not disapproved.'[44]

Both Kauṭilya and Vātsyayana are in favor of women doing some kind of job and getting proper wages. Kauṭilya recommends hard punishment for men indulging in any kind of extortion or bribery from such ladies. Both of these *Śāstrakāras* therefore also consider the situations of divorce in marriage.

The question whether a man is authorised to desert his wife at his will is to be determined by the concept of ownership. The question whether a man is owner of his wife and children is discussed by some of the *smṛtikāras*. Vijnāneśvara on Yaj. II.175 says – though a man cannot make a gift of his wife or children to other, still, he is the owner of his wife. Vīramitra also considers this view but differs with Vijnāeśvara. He says *svāmitva* here does not mean ownership, it just means controllability (*vaśitva*).

---

[41] गुरोः शिष्ये पितुः पुत्रे दम्पत्योः स्वामिभृत्ययोः ।
विरोधे तु मिथस्तेषां व्यवहारो न सिद्ध्यति । *Mitākṣarā* on *Yajnavalkyasmṛti*, II.32

[42] तदपि गुरुशिष्यादीनामात्यन्तिकप्रतिषेधपरं न भवति । तेषामपि कथश्चिद् व्यवहारस्य इष्टत्वात् । Ibid

[43] यदपि स्त्रीपुंसोः परस्परमर्थिप्रत्यथितया नृपसमक्षं व्यवहारो निषिद्धः तदपि प्रत्यक्षेण कर्णपरम्परया वा विदिते तयोः परस्परातिचारे दण्डादिना दम्पती निजमार्गे राज्ञा स्थापनीयौ ॥ *Mitākṣarā* on *Yajnavalkyasmṛti*, II.295

[44] विधाय वृत्तिं भार्यायाः प्रवसेत्कार्यवान्नरः ।
अवृत्तिकर्शिता हि स्त्री प्रदुष्येत्स्थितिमत्यपि ॥
विधाय प्रोषिते वृत्तिं जीवेन्नियममास्थिता ।
प्रोषिते त्वविधायैव जीवेच्छिल्पैरगर्हितैः ॥ *Manusmṛti*, IX.74-75

Manu and his followers provide easy ways to men to get rid of undesirable wives, but they do not extend the same kind of liberty to women. There are some other lawgivers who seem to be more liberal to married woman. They do allow some kind of scope for situations similar to divorce, none of them giving a word of solace or encouragement for a spouse seeking divorce even in dire need. Divorces amongst the married couples are not supposed to be good for the health of the society in the world-view of the law-givers; but then the possibilities of divorce taken as the last recourse do remain looming large on their horizons.

Bibliography

Aṣṭādaśasmṛti – compiled by Mihirchandra, Nag Prakashak, Delhi, 1990

Atharvaveda: Nag Prakashak, Delhi, 1994

Kauṇḍinyasmṛti – P. Sri Ramachandrudu, Hyderabad, 2004

Manusmṛtiḥ with com. *Manvarthamuktāvalī*; MLBD, 2000

Rgveda: (in five volumes) with Sāyaṇa's *bhāṣya*, Vaidik Samshodhan Mandal, Pune.

Vyavahāramayūkha: Nīlakaṇṭha, Text with Eng translation by P.V. Kane, Rashtriya Sanskrit Sansthan, New Delhi 2009

Yājñyavalkyasmṛti, with Mitākṣrā of Vijñāneśvara, ed. Narayan Ram Acharya, Nirnaya Sagar Press, 1949

The voice of verdict : Brij Kishor Swain, Choukhambha Publications, 2007

The Dharmaśātra : An Introductory Analysis : Brij Kishr Swain, Akshaya, Delhi, 2004

4

Unsung Documents: The Books Kept by Priests at Pilgrim Centres

B. N. Goswamy

MAY I SAY AT THE OUTSET how honoured I feel at being asked to speak in this series of lectures. My ignorance about manuscripts is of serious proportions. I shall, therefore, not go into what this Mission is doing at the moment, or what the range of manuscripts it is dealing with is. This has been spoken about by a number of people before me. I am going simply to confine myself to a very limited field, and I will go about, whatever I have to present, in a rather roundabout professorial manner, not directly addressing the issue but eventually landing up there. When I speak of the professorial manner I am reminded of a story somebody wrote about a gentleman from eastern Europe who, as a refugee, had landed up in Oxford after the Second World War. Not owning a wrist watch, and not very familiar with the

Note: This article does not represent a text sent in by Prof. Goswamy: It contains a partial recording of the Tattvabodha lecture he delivered on the subject at the National Mission for Manuscripts sometime back.

English language, he spotted on the street a Professor hastening towards the University, and simply asked him what time it was. The Professor stopped, thought for a while, and said: "Time? There, my friend, you have asked me a most profound question!" And then launched into a long winded lecture on the nature of Time. So, as an audience, you might have really landed yourselves into a situation like that. As a professor I might take very long indeed to come to what may be of marginal interest to you.

In any case, let's see where we can go with the subject of the documents of which I speak. These, I would like to add right now, are simply documents, and if they take the form of manuscripts, they do it rather surreptitiously. I am an art historian and I have little to do with these documents. But I will tell you how I landed with these records kept by priests at centres of pilgrimage..

Long years ago, around 1965 I recall, I was engaged with a search for finding more about the painters of the hill areas in northern India – the Pahari area as we might call it – than we did at that time. As we know, the world of Indian art is by and large a world of silence because there are hardly any records available. There are hardly any names of artists that have come down and the few that have hang about in the air like fire-flies in the night. You cannot catch them, and even when you have a name of any artist, sculptor or painter, it is just a name: very little else goes with it. The result is we do not have the critical wherewithal or the range of facts upon which art history is built. So we start with a major disadvantage: that of having very little information about painters who created these works while writing on the history of such art works. I had started on this search with a private theory of my own. In my view, styles of Indian paintings were not formed at courts but in the families of Indian artists. In order to gather a modicum of facts with the help of which I intended to build a theory, I needed to have as much information as possible on who the artists were, where did they come from, who did they relate themselves to, what court they belonged to; so on and so forth. At that time – this was some forty years ago – one was standing against a blank wall regarding these aspects.

I had had an exchange on this subject with a very distinguished, senior colleague of mine, W.G Archer, the Keeper of the Indian Section at Victoria & Albert Museum, London, and we had a number of friendly discussions – including many disagreements – about who possibly were the artists in the Pahari area that we were both interested in. In the course of our conversations one name kept cropping up repeatedly, a painter from the a little hill state called Guler, which is only a tiny blip on the map. This man, Nainsukh, had left some notes on some paintings, and some people, contemporaries or successors, had brought in his name in inscriptions on some works. I wanted to pursue this virtually unknown artist, for the works that carried his name were, in one word, simply superb.

But one was up against a wall. Where does one locate information? The surviving painters in the tradition had some information about their ancestors, but it was all un-documented. There was traditional memory, but it was shaky and one wanted to ground oral information in facts.

The year was 1965, as I recall. I was in Kurukshetra, a place of great pilgrimage and now the seat of a University. A friend of mine, Dr. Iqbal Nath Chaudhary, was teaching at the University there and I had gone to spend some days with him. During the day, my friend would, as usual, go off to teach, and I, sitting at his home, found time at my hands. It suddenly occurred to me one day that I could go and spend some time at the sacred tank called Suryakund in the town: a *tirtha* where the paṇḍās who are the traditional keepers of the records of visits of pilgrims, gather together. I headed to that particular spot then to enquire if any of the pandas had any records of painters in their *bahis*. Painters in the hills are called *chiteras* – a local version of the word, *chitrakar* – ; coming as they often did from the carpenter, or *tarkhan*, caste, they were also called *tarkhan chiteras*. This was the bare information with which I went to explore these records that I knew exist at places of pilgrimage. In the hills, there is a saying: 'If you do not go to Hardwar in your lifetime you will certainly go there when you are dead", meaning that that is where your ashes will be immersed in the Ganga.' So I was armed with the knowledge that almost every family visits Hardwar, and possibly some might have visited Kurukshetra on the way, at some point of time or the other. I also had a memory of when, long years ago, my father had taken me there for a visit, and had seen these records being used. So, there was hope in me that I might see something with the *pandas* at Kurukshetra as far as the *chiteras* of the Pahari area were concerned.

I did not know at that time that paṇḍās are extremely jealous of their records, for in some manner these are their bread and butter. So the first question asked of me when I approached the panda was, 'Why are you asking? Are you a *chitera*? If not, what is your interest?' Some of these questions, I found out, related to the fact that these records as genealogies of families are admissible in courts of law as evidence, particularly in property disputes and succession matters. Understandably, therefore, the paṇḍās hang on to them with good reason. At Kurukshetra, as I approached the pandas, I had to prove, through my local contacts, my *bonafides* as a researcher as also somehow assure the panda concerned that I would not misuse any information I got. One paṇḍā told me that they were no records on *chitrakars* alone: as a matter of routine, they were kept state-wise, region-wise, village-wise, and then according to the caste of the pilgrims, and so on. I began to get some idea of how to go about it, and having done that, and having given the impression that I was desperate, one panda out of sheer kindness I imagine, handed me a bahi, saying this related to the area – Kangra – that I was interested in. The *bahi*, like others of its kind, was a big tome (a slide will show that later). Saying that *this* is the *bahi*, the panda left for a while, adding that "you can try your luck". For the next three days, gingerly for I was still familiarizing myself with the system, I kept flipping through the leaves of the *bahi*, patiently, one by one, looking for a place – a village by the name of Samloti – from which some painters came as I had heard. On the fourth day, I flipped a leaf and suddenly sprang into sight a brief entry: "chitere, samloti ke", followed by a few lines containing one name after another. Needless to say, I was overwhelmed with excitement. They are there, I said to myself, in these books. From that time onwards, armed with this snippet of information I was doing nothing else in my life except travelling from *tīrtha* to *tīrtha*, *paṇḍā* to *paṇḍā*: Kurukshetra to Pehowa, on to Haridwar, Martand in Kashmir to Gaya in Bihar, Allahabad to Benaras. By the time I was done, and it took some years, I had what can be called a census of Pahari painters.

I would not say that you can turn into a historian in this manner, but at least for the limited end I had in sight, I had landed upon a string of facts with which I could develop my theory about styles and migrations and really how things worked in this chosen field. How it proceeded for me, and for the field of art history from this point on, is another story. Here I wish simply to say something about why do paṇḍās keep these records? How can these be accessed? What is the system that is followed in these tomes? The process is something that needs to be experienced first hand. But, for the sake of broad understanding, some things can be stated.

Over generations of time, families of *yajmanas* remain associated with paṇḍās who keep recording relevant information about 'their' families as time goes by. Let me reconstruct roughly the scene at a place, let us say like Haridwar. The moment you get off the bus, you are surrounded by a group of paṇḍās/munshis who know that you have come there on a pilgrimage. Everyone of them would shoot the same question at you: '*kahan ke basi?*' Meaning, where are you from? Not where have you travelled from but what is your native place? Taking my own example, I replied I am from Sargodha (now in Pakistan). Hearing this, from about twenty odd people who were surrounding me, around fifteen just disappeared, in search of other pilgrims. This because they did not have any records relating to Sargodha. The five or so who remained wanted to know further: "*kaun gaon*", meaning 'what village is your family native of?", obviously because Sargodha, in their reckoning, was a town and everyone originally came from a village. In reply, I said: "Sahiwal". "Aha", was the sound I heard. I could see that the information I was providing was being processed in their heads, essentially a process of elimination and confirmation. Further questions were shot: '*kaun jaat?*', meaning 'what is your caste'. I said Goswamy. By this time, only two of the pandas stayed with me with yet another question: 'kaun goswamy: "Goranwade, or Mulasantiye", referring obviously to two groups within the goswamy caste of Sahiwal. "Mulasantiye", I said, recalling the name of a prime ancestor that I had heard in my own family, from my mother. Light shining in his eyes, one of the pandas said, "I am going to recite some names; the minute you recognize one, stop me" All this purely from memory. He kept bringing up one name after another. The moment he uttered the name "Shankar Sahai", I said, a bit startled: 'that was the name of my grandfather". The search for the panda was over. He got hold of my hand, shoved me into a cycle-rickshaw, took me to the place of his work – meaning where they kept their bahis – unlocked a cupboard, pulled out one of the many tomes in it, flipped through its leaves very quickly, and shoved it towards me before I had barely recovered my breath. There they were, entry after entry relating to my entire family. I remember seeing my own misspelt 'signature' in English, dating back to the time when I was very young, had travelled to Haridwar with my father, and made that 'entry'. The feeling, the whole experience, was nothing short of magical. If one comes to think of it, the system that was developed, the enormity of the information that is there, the complete reliability of these records which sometimes stretch back to four hundred years, offers a remarkable field for further research and work.

As the system goes, if a painter, or any other person, from the hills has died and his son is taking his ashes to Hardwar for immersion, the son will definitely have to go to the paṇḍā of his own family. The paṇḍā would ask him a number of questions, plying him for information not only about him, his father and grandfather, but also other relatives. As much information as is possible and is of use to these records, would keep increasing with years.

Women, it needs to be mentioned, do not enter these records in the normal course. This would disappoint although not surprise, many, but one has to recognize that both the social system and these records were patrilinear. You are the son of so and so, who is the son of so and so: like this over a period of several hundred years these records have accumulated. And it is these records that I found to have been of extraordinarily use to me personally when I started looking for the kind of information at that point of time.

The records of the yajamanas and pilgrims apart, there is also much other information that the paṇḍās possess. Their private papers for instance, for they had a great deal of litigation amongst themselves for known causes. Questions arose when, for instance, who would inherit the bahis when a *panda* who had, say, four sons, died? In disputes of this kind of division of property – one bears in mind that these *bahis* were property proper for the pandas – they had to be pleaded before the established legal/judicial authority of the times. There is a sizeable amount of documentation of this kind that the paṇḍās possess I have seen *farmans*, *parwanas* and *parwanchas* of all kinds, in all types of languages and scripts with the paṇḍās: some of them I have reproduced in the books or articles I have published over the years.

The consistency and the authenticity of the *bahi* records of the *pandas*, which stretch far back into the past, need to be re-stated here perhaps. They are incontrovertible as evidence, for instance, when they contain signatures. That that are also consistent can be proven. When, for instance, starting from Guler in the hills, a person sets out on pilgrimage, comes to Kurukshetra, he comes and makes an entry in his own hand – or the paṇḍā does so for him –; from there he goes on to nearby Pehowa and, if you are lucky, you can locate his signature in the *bahi* of the paṇḍā at Pehowa who serves the same family; three days later you can locate the same signatures and name in the *bahī* at Hardwar because of the pilgrimage circuit that was commonly followed. One needs a slice of luck, but one bit of information can be verified against another: something that I, personally, have had the occasion to do.

Let me cite, at the end, how one specific search of mine for and in these records ended. Nainsukh, that great painter from Guler, was someone I was particularly interested in at one time. One of those years, when I was researching, I landed up in Hardwar, hoping to locate some information on him. I was staying at the Gita Bhawan; I knew, through some relations of mine, of two paṇḍās in Haridwars, the brothers Pandit Krishan Kumar and Ram Kumar, sons of Pandit Sardar Ram Rakha, a very prominent paṇḍā of Haridwar. When I located the family, I enquired from Sardar Ram Kumar if their family had kept the records of Guler, a question to which he said "yes". "Can I look at them", I asked, and he said, "We do have a *bahi* but it is lying in the court", obviously meaning that it was being referred to in a dispute. In practical terms, 'lying in the court" virtually means that it is now buried forever. I was greatly disappointed and the panda saw this. However, to my great good fortune, three short days later, the kind panda showed up at the door of the room in the Gita Bhawan where I was staying, a little cloth bag in his hand. All he said was: "*mujhe maloom hai ke aap bahut khoj rahein hain to main yeh nikal laya hoon.*" Meaning that I know you are looking for this record, so I have succeeded in bringing it out by some means. I could not believe my ears, for I do not know how he managed it. But he told me to go through it. On his part, he had no idea if the name of Nainsukh or someone else from his family, was in the *bahi*. Slowly, I started turning the pages and fortune smiled at me again. Suddenly, I experienced the same thrill that I had had at Kurukshetra years ago. I turned one folio, and there it was: a whole page-long entry in the hand of Nainsukh himself, not only giving information about himself, his father and grandfather, the date on which he had come, but also, oddly enough, the name of his maternal grandfather, maternal great grandfather so on. Also the words, in neat devanagari characters: "I am of the gotra sandal", adding that I have come here for this particular reason, and so on." What is more: being a painter, he must have picked up the very pen with which the *paṇḍā* must have been writing, and with it drew above the entry in his own hand a tiny little – about an inch and a half high – drawing of a subject entirely appropriate to the place, Haridwar: Shiva and Pārvatī seated on a *baghā-charma* (*tiger skin*) and Bhagīratha standing with folded hands in front of Śiva pleading with him to bring the Ganga from the heavens to the earth and bear its weight, exactly the miracle that Haridwar is known for. For me, it was a magical moment. What else can an art historian ask for? You not only find a nine line entry in the painter's own hand in Devanagari script giving the most precise information relating to his family and his visit: in addition, you also get a drawing.

On this very page, Nainsukh's entry was followed by a brief abstract of the entry in a different hand. This was common practice, for the paṇḍā himself had made the abstract, saying so and so came from such and such a place, etc. The panda must evidently felt the need to put Nainsukh's information in his own words and manner. All this I will have the pleasure of sharing with you when I turn to slides.

This, then, is the range of things I am talking about; this is the ambience of the place; these are the kind of people one deals with; these are the records they keep. You can make of it what you will. There, at places of pilgrimage, this body of wonderful information embedded in written records.

I might add that *pandas* are very focused but notoriously lazy as a people. If you think you can just walk up to them and ask them to open any particular *bahi*, that is unlikely to happen; you have to be exceedingly persistent. There is a Greek expression describing them in the *Gazetteer of the Kangra District* of 1881, which in translation reads as: "paṇḍās are a foul-mouthed, lazy, late rising, avaricious group". But, at the same time, these people are the custodians of some of the most valuable records that we have in this country. Allegedly we have no sense of history. But is that right? Perhaps in a strictly western sense it is true, but, in a different sense there is history written all over these pages; there is history which flows about; hovers in the air here. And all we have to do is to reach out, grasp it, and put it to our own use.

This presentation was followed by Prof. Goswamy showing a large number of slides of the *pandas* and their records. The slide-presentation, a selection of which is reproduced here, was prefaced with the following remarks.

There are pages in these manuscripts that are choc-a-block with information. Not all scripts are readable; some I might even be showing you upside down, for I am not too sure. There will also occasionally be a land grant with a seal like that on a *farman* or *parwancha*. Here we would see how a *paṇḍā* would, on a slow day, be sitting on the bank of the Suryakund with a *bahī* by his side, a *kalam* and a *dawat*, and a *soochi patra*. In one slide he can be seen holding up a page for me to photograph. When I became friendly with the paṇḍās of Kurukshetra they posed for me with the range of *bahīs* they had.

5

Representation of Knowledge in Sanskrit Tradition of Grammar

Rama Nath Sharma

I. *Ultimate Reality, Eternality and Tradition*

INDIAN KNOWLEDGE SYSTEM is traditional in nature. What is tradition? The word tradition can be explained, at best, as the core of a value system made manifest in practice (*vyavahāra*), especially in conduct. This core system of values is eternal (nitya) in nature. Now the question: what is nityatā 'eternality'. Our knowledge tradition looks at eternality as that which transcends time (*ananta*). That which is fixed (*dhruva*), does not come about or has any beginning (anādi), does not go through any modification (*vikāra*), and does not perish (*vinaśyati*). This is the reality (yathārtha) of knowledge (*jñāna*) in the Indian tradition. The anādi 'beginningless' aspect of ultimate reality represented in knowledge is presented in various formats for examples of the ṛk of the Vedas, the texts of the brāhmaṇas-āraṇyakas, and more importantly the Upaniṣads, generally called Vedānta. This ultimate reality transcends time (*kāla*) since it does not perish. Note also here that kāla 'time' itself is eternal (*nitya*), and in this sense transcends kāla. Let us see what kāla is:

Time is a full vessel which never goes empty, only spills. He has gathered together all beings that are. He has passed through all gathered beings: He who was father has become their son; There is no glory higher than this. The passing moments, present and future, by him set swinging, are reckoned out in due proportions. This is the eternal Time: that which cannot be measured. What can be measured is a mere manifest of the eternal Time: our time, the temporal time. When (the eternal time) he has performed this work of creation, he ceases; then enters into unions of beings with his Being. The temporal time is also *nitya* but *pravāha-nitya*. This is what in simple terms is tradition (*paramparā*). Consider Gaṅgā which is *nitya*, never born, not dying, fixed, unmodified, not going through any modification. Consider *himālayād gaṅgā prabhavati* where the word the *kāraka* term *apādāna* is assigned to himālaya, and *apādāne pañcamī* assigns the second triplet of nominal endings to express this relationship to yield *himālayāt*. Patañjali interprets the word *prabhava* as *prathamaṃ darśanam* 'first appearance', and not the origin, or birth. The gaṅgā of our times is nitya but *pravāha-nitya* 'eternal in the flow of time and place'.

Let us now return to *sṛṣṭi* which is *nitya*, and so is the time (kāla). But within the perspective of Time we find *ṣṛṣṭi* in cycles of *ṣṛṣṭi* 'creation', *pralaya* 'dissolution' and *ṣṛṣṭi* 'creation', again. There are a quite a few Sūktas of the Ṛgveda, the most ancient record available for mankind, which deal with creation. I shall here deal here with just two: the Nāsadīya and the Puruṣa-sūkta. The nāsadīya reveals to us what existed yet did not at the beginning of the beginning-less beginning:

There existed no being, nor did any non-being then; no air, no sky beyond that. What was that which covered, and what, and where, under whose protection was there that deep unfathomable water? There was no mortality, and hence no immortality. There was no indication of neither night, nor day. There was nothing yet there was HE (that), alone, who breathed with no wind, with his own will-power. No other thing than that existed beyond: darkness was that which darkness covered before. This all was water with no indication of it whatsoever. That which was there to come about, was covered with void (śūnya). HE, alone, by power of his tapas, came into being. Desire was there in him before, the first seed of thought that it was. In their hearts, searching with their wisdom, the sages found their bonds with being, in the non-being. The force of creation, the great vital energy, was there. Up above was the power of will, below was the discipline (svadhā). Who could know here for sure, who could further explain, whence this creation came about, and progressing to where on this side. Gods were born with progression of creation. Who then knew from whence this creation arose. Did he create, or did he not. HE who presides over it in the highest heaven, HE alone for sure knows, or may be HE does not know.

The force of creation, the power of tapas, the great vital energy, the power of will, His will, above, the discipline below, this is what came into being. How can we reconcile the opposites of these observations of the nāsadīya. The key is the very word nāsat, a combination of na + asat where asat is na sat = non-existence and na asat is non-non-existence, or similar to but different from existence. There are two negations in Sanskrit, *prasajya* 'absolute' and *paryudāsa* 'similar to but different from (*tadbhinna-tatsadṛśa*)'.

Now let us see what existed but did not. The first verse says there was no being, there was no non-being. Yet there He was breathing without wind. There was no night, nor day, yet there was void, darkness covered with darkness. It was the power of tapas which brought desire in him; the first seeds of thought which turned into vital energy, the great force of creation. The sages in their hearts, searching through their wisdom found their bond in the non-being. How was this made possible? By power of will resulting out of tapas, and discipline (svadhā). This is where and when the non-being came into being. This is where gods and sages received their state of existence to establish their bond with him by their tapas, wisdom, and discipline. This is the point of progression for creation. The creation which proceeds from what we know as Brahma, via the Puruṣa-sūkta.

When the non-being came into being, gods and sages with their tapas, wisdom and discipline, performed the sacrifice by means of the sacrifice, with puruṣa serving as the offering. From that sacrifice, with its invocation made to the MAN within all, Ṛk and Sāman hymns were revealed; from that came about the chandas (*gāyatrī*), and from that came about the Yajus'. Moon sprung from his mind; Sun from his eyes; from his mouth were born Indra and Agni; from his breathing the wind came about (the Prāṇa). From his navel came about the antarikṣa (the world in between); from his head unfurled the sky; from his feet came the earth, from his ears the directions; this is how the worlds were fashioned out, all. There were seven circles; three-times seven were made the samidh 'sacrificial stick'. With sacrifice the gods sacrificed; these were the first (practices of) dharma (neuter, acts which accrue merit, and by means of which, one is sustained); then these exalted ones ascended to the heaven where gods who preceded, and other exalted ones, already lived. What came about went back and disappeared into what it came about from, and came about once again when the wheels of creation were set in motion after the dissolution. Whatever went back into and came about from in the cycle of creation is the ultimate reality the Brahman.

Before we move to the understanding of the ultimate reality, the Brahman, let us reflect on one very important observation of the Puruṣa-sūkta: *tāni dharmāṇi prathamānyāsan* 'those were the primordial dharmas'. What is dharma? The word dharma is explained as:

> *dhriyate anena dharati iti vā* 'that by means of which (one's) life is sustained, or that which sustaines (one's life)'.

A much more modern understanding of the word dharma as 'religion' is nothing but a misnomer, and hence should be rejected. The word dharma, from all traditional considerations, could best be understood as the value system, where value could better be interpreted as virtue. I shall here not go into dharma which manifests in Truth (satya) and which in turn, manifests in the conduct of us mortals in thirteen facets: truth (satya), non-violence (ahiṃsā), equality (samatā), steadfastness (dhairya), discipline (yoga), etc. This dharma protects us but only when we protect the dharma (*dharmo rakṣati rakṣitaḥ*). When dharma becomes institutionalized and it is added on with directives of do's (vidhi) and don'ts (niṣedha), it becomes religion. The choice of engaging in actions marked with good and bad deeds (sukṛta-duṣkṛta), which, in turn, accrue merits (puṇya) and demerits (pāpa), is then largely controlled by the do's and don's of the institutionalized dharma, better called religion. It also in many ways sets its control on the free flowing dharma in the flow of time and space (pravāha-nitya). This brings forth a new meaning to tradition. But what happens to Truth? Truth (dharma) in this state of pravāha-nityatā, finds three faces: my face of truth, your face of truth and his face of truth. In between these three faces of truth there is a fourth: the true face of truths own (his) face. The problem is: we always strive to see the face of truth from behind, the back of Truth. This is why we say: true face of truth can never be seen. I shall here mention the story of Kaushika Brāhmaṇa who was prompted by a housewife to go to Mithila and learn the the truth about dharma. This most telling story is couched in the the Mahābhārata in the format of Upākhyāna where the Dharmavyādha tells it all about dharma by way of the conduct of his family: father-mother, wife and children.

Knowledge in the Sanskrit tradition is represented in the format of the ṛk of the Vedas (śruti), the recall based format of the smṛtis, in the mostly prose format of the Upaniṣads. A great body of knowledge is represented in the sūtra format of the Mlmāṃsā, Nyāya, Sāṃkhya, Yoga, Dharma, and Vyākaraṇa disciplines of knowledge. This all is represented within the perspective of *nityatā* 'eternality, both fixed (kūṭastha) and one caught in the flow of time and space (pravāha-nityatā). Knowledge is represented in śabda which is manifest vāk 'speech'. Let us see how the knowledge capturing the ultimate reality brahma is represented in *śabda*, the manifest vāk.

II. *Brahma and śabdabrahma*

Bhartṛhari considers Brahma as the word-essence (śabda-tattva) from whence the creation of the worlds proceeds, by way of appearance (vivarta) of objects.

anādinidhanaṃ brahma śabdatattvaṃ yadakṣaram/
vivartate' rthabhāvena prakriyā jagato yataḥ //VP:I: 1 //

Brahma is beyond the scope of birth and death. It is ātman, especially in view of diversity in forms (*vṛhatvād vṛṃhaṇtvāc ca ātmā brahmeti gīyate*). That which exists all the time is ātman (*atati satataṃ gacchatīti*). This is brahmatattva, consciousness (cetana), and self-illuminating jñāna. The śruti says *vijñānam ānandaṃ Brahma*, pure knowledge, and bliss. The śruti supports vijñāna as the form of Brahma. This brahma or ātmā is witness to all. That is, it serves as the source of all objects (padārtha) at all times, past, present and future. There is no disappearance (abhāva) of it ever. For, it is the source of all there is, or there comes about, or returns there to. The śruti says, *yato vā imāni bhūtāni yāyante yena jātāni jīvanti yataḥ prayanti abhisamaviśanti.*

Veda is the primary vivarta of Brahman, and also its primary symbol (anukāra). Veda is one but has been handed down to us in many recensions by the sages (ṛṣis). One can also say that Veda is the pratipādaka 'the manifest' and Brahman is pratipādya 'that which is made manifest'.

prāptyupāyo' nukāraśca tasya vedo maharṣibhiḥ /
eko' pyanekavartmeva samāmnātaḥ pṛthakpṛthak // VP I:5//

The idea of Brahman and Śabda-brahman is not based on any difference between the two. As the practice of *dāna* 'giving', and conduct of *tapas* 'austerity' and *brahmacarya* 'celebacy' facilitates *abhyudaya* 'auspicious rise', that same way one attains Brahma with purity of mind attained by studying the Veda, and by following the conduct approved by the Veda. The brahman of the Vedāntin can thus be attained by means of Veda. Further, for reasons of being pervasive, and also because of its growth in diversity, the ātman itself is called brahman. Note that Brahman is *kūṭastha-nitya* 'eternally fixed', as against ātman which, identified with Brahman as its manifestation, is bounded with time and space. It still is nitya 'eternal' but in the flow of time and space (pravāha-nitya). When this same brahman of the ātman is made manifest by articulated sounds it is called the śabda-brahman 'word, the supreme', not any different from the brahman of the Vedāntin.

If one looks at it in view of the śruti, i.e., *tasya bhāsā sarvam idaṃ vibhāti* 'this all glows with his light', we understand that Brahman is the source of all illuminations. When we perceive the sattā 'existence' of a ghaṭa 'jar' with our eyes, etc., we find that this same Brahman is making the *ghaṭa* manifest with his accompanying glow. When we say *ayaṃ ghaṭaḥ* 'this is a jar', this *ghaṭa* is made manifest by the articulated sound. How? It is by the *sphoṭa* of the articulated sound that meaning of *ghaṭa* is cognized. There is thus no difference between the brahman of the Vedāntin and the Śabda-brahman. There will be duality (dvaita) if one accepts them as two different entities. This would then go against the view of the śruti as voiced in ekam evādvitīyam 'this indeed is uniquely one' and neha *nānāsti kiṃcana* 'there is nothing different here'. Bhartṛhari has indicated his agreement with the ideas of Brahman and māyā, etc., of the Vedāntin by accepting the idea of vivarta, and by showing the same Brahman as different by way of difference (bheda) of power (śakti). As this entire cosmos is made manifest by power of differential of Brahman the eternal, so is this universe of word made manifest by power of differential of Śabda-brahman. This universe of words consists of different objects expressing different experiences. All differentiations consisting of all experiences and all experience itself along with words expressive of the objects of experience proceed from the Śabda-brahman, identical with the Brhaman (Iyer, Bhartṛhari, p. 58). This is the eternal and undifferentiated Śabda-brahman which is within all of us. Ambākartī (on VP I:1) interprets *prakriyā jagato yataḥ* as *jagato mūlabhūtasya vedasya* 'of the Veda which is at the root of the appearance of the universe'. The word *prakriyā* is interpreted in the sense *prathamam utpattiḥ* 'first coming into existence of'. This fits neatly into the order of things where Veda is the first appearance (vivarta) of Brahman, thereby constituting the śabdabrahman from whence the universe first comes about. It is by lakṣaṇā that jagat is accepted here as denoting the Veda, the origin of jagat. Not accepting this would involve *punarukti-doṣa* 'the fault of repetition' in stating the origin of jagat stated by *vivartato' rthabhāvena*, again by *prakriyā jagato yataḥ*. Accepting the origin of the Veda first would put everything in perspective as follows: The Brahman, the word-principle (śabda-tatva) Brahman, becomes manifest by way of meaning, and what comes at the root of this expatiated Śabda-brahman is the Veda. This is what is stipulated by part of the kārikā-verse *chandobhya eva prathamam idaṃ viśvaṃ vyavartata* 'it is the chandas 'Veda' from whence this universe came about'.

Whether or not the Vivartin brahma is the preserver, nourisher, or whether he is the cause of dissolution is not clearly stated. It is hinted though that preservation and dissolution of this jagat can also be accepted at his hands. For, as long as the rope is there the snake is there. This is how the rope preserves the snake. But removal of darkness brings disappearance of snake into the rope. This is how the dissolution of jagat could be understood. This is how the process of jagat appears from Brahma, and disappears back into him. A question arises whether Brahma of the śruti and the Śabda-brahma are the same, or not the same. Recall that parā originates in the brahman and is also identified with Śabda-brahma. If this is accepted then parā could not be accepted anādi 'with no beginning'. There is yet another objection. If the origin of parā is stated then Śabda-brahma would be accepted as the vivarta of the *anādinidhana* 'beginningless-endless'. But since there is no vivarta of vivarta, there would not be any sṛṣṭi from the Śabda-brahman. That is, jagat would be accepted as the vivarta of the anādinidhana, śrutisiddha Brahma but it could not be accepted as the vivarta of the Śabda-brahman. But such an objection is not valid. For, nescience (avidyā) is the cause of vivarta, and cetana-Brahma alone, is the substratum (adhiṣṭhāna) of avidyā. What comes as vivarta in the form of jagat is the avidyā located within the brahma. This is why jagat also remains within its cause, the avidyā located within the Brahma.

Nāgeśa (Mañjūṣā) not only considers parā as the *upādāna kāraṇa* of jagat, but also also accepts it as *sarvagata* 'all pervasive'. In order to accept parā as the upādāna kāraṇa of jagat, the principle of sṛṣṭi proceeding from śabda has to be accepted. This is what the śruti also supports:

sa bhūr iti vyāharat sa bhūmim asṛjat
'HE uttered bhū, (and thus) created the Earth'

A sṛṣṭi which proceeds from śabda after dissolution (pralaya) begins with the Veda. From that point on sṛṣṭi proceeds from the Śabda which is Veda. This is why Nāgeśa considers parā, paśyantī and madhyamā the manifest of Praṇava. These three states of vāk are also identified as extremely subtle, subtler and subtle. Praṇava or Omkāra is the subtle Veda. It is stated that the EARTH was created by uttering bhūḥ. Since parā falls within the scope of manas, the subtle articulation happens to be in the paśyantī vāk. Since the names parā, paśyantī, madhyamā, etc., relate to expression of the same Brahma-tattva at different places, the subtle articulation of bhū in the madhyamā which creates bhū 'earth' is directly relatable to parā. This way, Śabda-brahma is accepted as the source from whence sṛṣṭi proceeds. Note here that Brahma is nitya 'eternal', and yet considering HIS expression at the levels of mūlādhāra, etc., the use of the word utpatti is made relative to parā and paśyantī.

III. *Representation of Knowledge in the Sūtra Format of Śabda*

catvāri śṛṅgā trayo asya pādā
dve śīrṣe sapta hastāso asya/
tridhā baddho vṛṣabho roravīti
maho devo martyā āviveśa//

Indian theorists of language believe in the divine origin of speech (vāk). They begin with something which is not only physical and direct (pratyakṣa) but is also received by auditory instrumentalities and, in the process, is perceived by buddhi 'high intelligence.' Perception by *buddhi* is the function of mind (manas). Reception by auditory instrumentalities is associated with the function of vital air (prāṇa). It is *buddhi* which mediates between manas and prāṇa, and as a result, vāk, i.e, *buddhyārūḍha-śabda* 'word-on-mind,' comes into articulation. This articulation of vāk has its source in nāda (noise) which, at the initiation of prāṇa and through efforts (prayatna) of karaṇas 'speech-organs' at specific places (sthāna) results in dhvani 'sound', itself a modification (vikāra) of outgoing lung-air (śvasana). It is stated that vāk is a modified form of prāṇa, immobile, located at the mūlādhāra in the form of bindu encompassing the śabda-Brahman and is most commonly known as primary speech (parā-vāk). A modification of this vāk by the time it reaches nābhi 'navel' is known as paśyantī, though still internal and perceived only by mind. This same internal vāk, again only perceived by mind, is known as intermediate (madhyamā) when it reaches the heart (hṛt). When reaching the oral cavity and hitting the dome of the mouth it gets yet another modified name (vaikharī). This is what is commonly known as fully externalized speech, i.e., dhvani, and this is what the listener receives with his auditory instrumentalities. It is this same dhvani which strikes the inner years of the listeners and is perceived by his buddhi where pratibhā mediates to bring about cognition, by way of pratibhā the seven hands a prathamā, etc., nominal endings (vibhakti).

The subject matter (upajīvya) of grammar, i.e., speech (vāk), itself has been accorded a divine status. The tradition claims that vāk is the essence of man and Vedic ṛk is the essence of vāk. Bhartṛhari (6 AD), in his Vākyapadīyam, reveres grammar as a smṛti 'canonical code,' and recognizes the Vyākaraṇamahābhāṣya (Mbh.) of Patañjali (2 B.C.) as the source for knowledge of all theoretical constructs. The Brāhmaṇas, Saṃhitās, Upaniṣads and earlier classical literary texts such as the Mahābhārata and the Rāmāyaṇa, all attest to the fact that vyākaraṇa, by their time, had already become a well-established discipline of learning. Patañjali recognizes that a brāhmaṇa initiate, after his initiation, was required to study grammar. It comes as no surprise then to see grammar accepted as one of the Vedāṅgas, a field of study to be pursued as a must. Note that Patañjali, while stating that grammar was included in the curriculum of young Brāhmaṇa initiates, uses the expression purākalpa etad āsīt 'it was like this in ancient times.'

The utterances of Vedic Sanskrit formed the basis for *śabdopadeśa* 'instruction about words' by Vedic Indians first with extraction of individual constituent padas 'fully derived words' from continuous indivisible (akhaṇḍa) utterances and then subjecting the extracted pada to analysis in terms of bases (prakṛti) and affixes (pratyaya). This extraction of individual padas was aptly named padapāṭha 'recitation of individual padas,' as against the more commonly available indivisible recitation known as the saṃhitāpāṭha 'recitation of Vedic utterances with no extraction of individual padas from their continuous recitation in close proximity (saṃhitā).' This systematic extraction of individual padas from the saṃhitā texts required, at the least, some understanding of grammatical categories and operations with reference to which individual padas could be established. Given the nature and importance of the Vedic texts it is no surprise that linguistic studies in ancient India centered around them. The Prātiśākhyas are considered Vedic grammars, though some of them also include discussion on meters (chandas) and phonetics (śikṣā). It is very well known that ancient Indians excelled in their study of phonetics, and phonology. There was also a brief period when intellectual endeavors were focused on etymological explanations (nirvacana). Yāska's Nirukta is a classic example of nirvacana. Durgācārya (Mīmāṃsaka I:261–262), claims that there were fourteen texts of the Nirukta (caturdaśaprabhedam). Yāska himself mentions 13, fourteen scholars. Note that Nirukta is a commentary on Nighaṇṭu which, by itself is a dictionary of Vedic words presented in three sections. The first section, namely naighaṇṭuka, is a collection of 1341 synonyms. The second section is called naigama with 279 words of multiple meanings and uncertain etymology. The third section is daivata with 151 names of divinities. This brings the total number of words in Nighaṇṭu to 1771.

There are references in Pāṇini to five kinds of texts which I suspect all made representation of grammatical knowledge:

i. *dṛṣṭa* 'seen, revealed': a text which is not man made (apauruṣeya) but is revealed, instead. Consider 4.2.7 *dṛṣṭaṃ sāma* 'revelation of sāman hymn' and 4.2.8 *vāmadevāḍ ḍyaḍḍyau ca 'tha taddhita* affixes Ḍyaḍ and Ḍyau occur after the syntactically related nominal stem ending in the tṛtīyā 'instrumental,' namely Vāmadeva, when the derivative denotes 'revelation of sāman received by Vāmadeva;

ii. *prokta* 'stated with excellence': a text which is made for explanation to students (4.3.10 tena proktam 'elucidated with excellence by him'). Note that a prokta text could be both an original text, or one made by some other scholar. For example, pāṇininā proktaṃ pāṇinīyam, anyena proktā māthureṇa proktā māthurī vṛttiḥ 'a text which was elucidated by Pāṇini; made by someone elucidated by Māthura';
iii. *upajñāta*, 'a text which was perceived by the author by his own intellect.' Mīmāṃsaka informs that in such texts one includes the description of some aspect of a prokta text in an entirely brilliant way;
iv. *kṛta*, a text which is made by the author in its entirety;
v. *vyākhyāna*, a text which explains and elucidates a text with notes and commentaries.

The *Aṣṭādhyāyī* of Pāṇini is a text of the prokta 'stated with excellence' style. A careful look at the developmental aspect of representation of knowledge in ancient India reveals a sustained effort towards structuring knowledge into a format most conducive, not only toward maintaining rigor and preserving content, but also toward explaining it for those who most needed to be enlightened. History of India in general, and her intellectual history in particular, could not have changed this drastically for a better had it not been due to the birth of the Buddha. The discipline of grammar similar to many other branches of learning, for example Mīmāṃsā, Sāṃkhya, Nyāya, and the Śrauta, Gṛhya and Kalpa Sūtras, got its knowledge represented in the format of the sūtra style (Sharma, 2002: 1–2). Pāṇini's Aṣṭādhyāyī, i.e., the recitation of his sūtras (sūtrapāṭha), excelled all competition in the field. Looking at the excellence of the *Aṣṭādhyāyī* as a grammatical system one would rightly assume that the *Aṣṭādhyāyī* of Pāṇini must have developed as part of a very rich grammatical tradition.

Aṣṭādhyāyī sūtra was considered a formulaic statement representing a thread of idea with brevity and precision (Limaye 1974:36). Its goal was to capture generalizations extracted from usage, and facilitate derivation of correct words. But this brevity and precision was not accomplished at the expense of clarity. Since grammatical rules were formulated with brevity, and within the perspective of a meta-theory, sūtras certainly needed explanations. It is to explain a sūtra with a statement which best captured the true intent of its formulator that the development of another style of literature, namely vṛtti, could not be helped. *Aṣṭādhyāyī* vṛtti 'paraphrase' statement was keyed into a sūtra to facilitate proper understanding of the sūtra, again with brevity. *Aṣṭādhyāyī* vṛtti thus accepted a sūtra as its focus, or symbol (pratīka), for formulation of its statement.

Since a correct interpretation of sūtras demanded extreme caution in weighing questions of under-application, over-application, and in extremely few instances no application at all, a vṛtti was subjected to deeper scrutiny. This gave rise to a vast body of very brief and focused statements generally known as vārttikas. A vārtika examined a sūtra from the express point of view of what is stated (ukta) by a rule, what is not stated (anukta) by a rule, and what has been poorly stated (durukta), by a rule (*uktānuktadrukta-cintakatvam vārttikatvam*). A fairly substantial number of vārttikas which were formulated by Kātyāyana on the sūtras of Pāṇini are found in the *Vyākaraṇa-mahābhāṣya* of Patañjali. These vārttikas have become synonymous with what we know as vārttikas. A vārttika, by way of accepting a sūtra as its focus, puts a sūtra to test.

The discourse style of the Mahābhāṣya accepts vārttikas as pratīka 'focus (symbol)' and offers its deliberations (vyākhyāna) by first introducing a topic and then discussing the same in view of questions (praśna), answers (uttara), refutations (ākṣepa) and resolutions (samādhāna), all illustrated with examples (udāharaṇa) and counter-examples (pratyudāharaṇa). The bhāṣya thus takes the vārttika as its pratika 'focus' and presents its discussion of a sūtra in view of examples and counter-examples. A bhāṣya thus, by way of accepting a vārttika as its focus, again puts a sūtra to test. This interlocking dependency of focus on sūtra, vṛtti and bhāṣya also became the main style of representation of knowledge in many other branches of learning in ancient India (Sharma 2002:6).

The *Vyākaraṇa-mahābhaṣya* of Patañjali is considered the first ever serious attempt to present a successful theory of linguistics, especially grammar. These focus-driven deliberations also gave rise to two other kinds of texts which, in the field of grammar, are recognized as: prakriyā and siddhānta. The prakriyā texts aim on presenting the corpus of the sūtras of Pāṇini in a new arrangement, so that placement of rules, their explanations and illustrations could prove most conducive to applied aspect of grammatical derivation (prakriyā). The tradition of prakriyā texts begins with the *Rūpāvatāra* of Dharmakīrti followed by the *Prakriyā-kaumudī* of Rāmacandra. It reaches its peak in the *Siddhānta-kaumudī* of Bhaṭṭoji Dīkṣita which, in turn becomes the source for an abridged *Sārasiddhāntakaumudī* and a middle-length *Madhyasiddānt-kaumudī*, both made by Varadarāja. Varadarāja's own Laghu-kaumudī brings this rich tradition of prakriyā to a full circle.

The siddhānta texts focused more on topics of theoretical interest and presented them in such an in-depth analytical manner that set standards of grammar in the tradition of Pāṇini. The *Vākyapadīya* of Bhartṛhari is the single most important text on Philosophy of Language. Bhartṛhari accepts that all theoretical constructs of the tradition of Pāṇini have their source in the Mahābhāṣya of Patañjali. Pāṇini, Kātyāyana and Patañjali are revered as three sages, and according to the dictum of *yathottaraṃ munīnāṃ prāmāṇyam*, each subsequent sage enjoys relatively greater authority pramāṇa, making Patañjali the supreme authority in matters pertaining to Pāṇini. Bhaṭṭoji Dīkṣita, Kauṇḍa Bhaṭṭa and Nāgeśa are three important authors in the development of the Siddhānta literature. All these siddhānta texts, by their own admission, discuss and explain the principles established by the *Vyākaraṇa-mahābhāṣya* of Patañjali.

The *Vākyapadīya* (VP) of Bhartṛhari (AD 5), *Vaiyakarana-siddhāntakārikā* of Bhaṭṭoji Dīkṣita, *Vaiyākaranabhūṣana* of Kaunḍabhaṭṭa (AD 17), itself being a commentary on the *Vaiyakaranasiddhantakarika* of Bhattoji Dīksita, and *Vaiyākaraṇasiddhāntamañjūṣā* of Nageśabhaṭṭa (Nageśa; AD 17-18), with a short and very short (laghu; paramalaghu) version, are important text of the Siddhānta literature. Bhaṭṭoji Dīkṣita's *Śabda-kaustubha* and Nāgeśa's *Laghu* and *Bṛhacchabdenduśekhara*, and *Paribhāṣenduśekhara* (PŚ) are other important texts on issues in Siddhānta.

kiṃcit sāmānyaviśeṣavat lakṣaṇaṃ pravartyam yenālpena yatnena mahato mahataḥ śabdaughān pratipadyeran /

Mahābhāṣya (I:6)

It has been explained that the Sanskrit grammatical tradition is a focus driven tradition where representation of linguistic knowledge has been made in the text formats of sūtra, vṛtti, vārttika, bhāṣya, prakriyā and siddhānta. It should be noted that the text of a preceding format style serves as focus for the text of the succeeding format style. We thus will accept that a sūtra has word (śabda) as its focus. A vṛtti will similarly have the sūtra-pāṭha (SP) as its focus. For a bhāṣya discussion we must also have a vārttika as focus. A sūtra, along with its vṛtti and related vārttikas, should form the focus for prakriyā texts. A siddhānta text generally has the final view of the Vyākaraṇa-mahabhāṣya of Patañjali as its focus, especially for offering detailed formulations, and facilitating a comparatively better understanding. I shall next present the developmental history of Sanskrit grammatical tradition under subsections the Sūtra-pāṭha, the Vyākaraṇa-mahābhāṣya of Patañjali, Vṛtti, Prakriyā and Siddhānta. I shall discuss the Mahābhāṣya after a short introduction to the Sūtra-pāṭha before the Vṛtti, Prakriyā and Siddhānta literature, in this order simply because Patañjali enjoys the most authority in the tradition. Besides, the *Vyākaraṇa-mahābhāṣya* of Patañjali includes discussions on every aspect of grammatical literature of the three sages (trimuni).

Pāṇini appears with his *Aṣṭādhyāyī* (henceforth the A) at a stage when intellectual pursuits of speech theoreticians had moved to the stage of analyzing words as part of utterances, used as means of communicating ideas. That Pāṇini chose to formulate a limited body of serially and/or otherwise ordered limited number of sūtras to account for the infinity of utterances of the Sanskrit language was no accident. For, the sūtra-style of describing reality in the realm of knowledge had become well-established. It is true that Pāṇini's A stands as the single most remarkable treatise in the field of grammatical speculation. However, it will be a mistake to believe that the technique of capturing generalizations, i.e., of (usage of) speech by formulating general (sāmānya) rules of grammar (lakṣaṇa) along with related particulars (viśeṣa) which necessarily include exceptions (apavāda) and negations (pratiṣedha), was something newly developed by Pāṇini. Instead, his A developed as a remarkable body of sūtras presenting the most complete grammar of the Sanskrit language, or for that matter, of any past or present language of the world, as what can now be called the culmination of a rich tradition of grammatical speculation. A tradition which may have started with the padapāṭha technique of textual rendition as opposed to a corresponding saṃhitāpāṭha and which after a brief preoccupation with the etymologies of individual words and utterances may have moved toward preparing some solid foundations. It is claimed, and to a large extent correctly, that there were eighty five known grammarians prior to Pāṇini. We find references in the A to pre-Pāṇinian grammarians, for example, Āpiśali, Kāśyapa, Gārgya, Gālava, Bhāradvāja and Śākaṭāyana, whose works constituted the formative stages of this aspect of grammatical speculation. Unfortunately, the works of these grammarians, except for a few references, are not available.

A question is raised whether grammar should teach correct words, incorrect words, or correct and incorrect words both. Since a single word has many corrupt counterparts, and also since teaching of correct words is comparatively more economical, grammar teaches correct words. Consider *gauḥ* which has many corrupt (apabhraṃśa) counterparts, for example *gāvī,* goṇī, gotā, gopotalikā, etc. Besides grammar should teach only what is desired (iṣṭa). How should this teaching of correct words proceed? Teaching words by way of their individual enumeration, namely pratipada-pāṭha, is here mentioned as one of the methods used by Bṛhaspati, an ideal teacher, for teaching grammar to Indra, an ideal student. But this method of studying grammar was pursued for a thousand heavenly years with no end in sight. What to talk of today when, if a person lives for long, he only lives for a hundred years. Patañjali concludes that this method of pratipada-pāṭha is no means at all (*anabhyupāya eṣa*).

Patañjali again raises the question, 'how else should words be understood.' He states that rules with general and particular properties be formulated so that this vast ocean of words could be understood with little effort. A general (utsarga) rule is to be formulated based on generalization to which a particular (viśeṣa) rule could be related by way of being an exception (apavāda). Consider, for example, 3.2.1 *karmaṇy* aṇ 'affix a*Ṇ* is introduced after a verbal root when used in construction with a pada denoting object (karman), whose related exception is 3.2.3 *āto' nupasarge kaḥ* 'affix *Ka* is introduced after a verbal root ending in *–ā*, and not used with any pre-verb, when a pada denoting *karman* occurs in construction.' A question is then raised about the meaning of constituent words which enter into the formulation of general and particular rules. That is, whether their meaning is jāti 'class' or individual (vyakti). It is both since the Ācārya formulates his rules both ways (ubhayathā). Consider 1.2.58 *jātyākhyāyām ekasmin bahuvacanam anyatarasyām* and 1.2.64 *sarūpāṇām ekaśeṣa ekavibhaktau.*

Patañjali next introduces a statement of his own as focus: *siddhe śabdārthasambandhe*, whereby śabda, artha and śabdārtha-sambandha are considered nitya 'permanent.' It is further stated that nitya is not only that which stays fixed (avicāli), does not go through modification (vikāra), or does not get destroyed (naśyati). It is also that whose essence (tatva) stays even after it goes through destruction. Consider the property (dharma) of pot-ness (ghaṭatva) which remains even after the pot (ghaṭa) is destroyed. That is, *jāti* 'class property' remains even after *vyakti* 'individual' gets destroyed. But how is it known that śabda, artha and śabdārtha-sambandha are nitya? We know it from loka 'usage.' That is, it is not known from grammatical analysis. A grammarian teaches śabda-sādhutva 'correctness of words.' Knowledge of śabdārtha 'word meaning'. It is in this context that Patañjali introduces the concept of nityatā 'eternality.' That which stay fixed (dhruva), does not go through any modification and does not get destroyed is called kūṭastha-nitya. The other is called pravāha-nitya 'eternal in flow.' Simply put, the 'the eternal in flow' is one bounded by time and space (deśa-kāla). It should be remembered here that kāla itself shares the two aspects of eternal. Nāgeśa explains nitya as akṛtaka 'not brought about,' i.e., 'that which cannot be brought about, produced or affected by grammar (vyākaraṇāniṣpādyatva).' Kaityaṭa (Pradīpa under 3.4.67 *kartari kṛt*) states that Pāṇini formulated his grammar by accepting *śabdārtha-sambandha* as eternal. In view of *pravāhanityatā* it can be viewed as arbitrariness.

A grammarian does not have any control over the goal of his analysis (lakṣya). He enjoys control over his rules (lakṣaṇa), insofar as they can capture the usage. Rules of grammar are formulated for capturing the nature of usage and not to dictate the reality of usage. Rules of grammar are subservient to reality of usage (*lakṣyaparatantratvāt lakṣaṇaṇasya,* Pradīpa 5.2.80). Word, meaning and their relationship exists prior to the formulation of grammar; their understanding does not have to necessarily come from grammar. Grammatical analysis informs about correctness of words (śabda-sādhutva); it does not control correctness. Consider someone going to a potter's and asking him, 'make a pot, I wish to use it.' This may be the reality of the outside world. It certainly is not true in the world of grammar. It is 'not like the one who, wishing to make use of a pot, goes to the pot-maker and says: "Make me a pot, I am going to make use of it," does one who, wishing to use words, go to the grammarians and say: "Make (me) words, I am going to use them." This clearly establishes the *Aṣṭādhyāyī* of Pāṇini as a grammar which could not be called prescriptive. When Pāṇini states 6.1.77 *iko yaṇ aci* 'let *iK* be replaced with *yaṆ* when *aC* follows,' he does not dictate this replacement (Bhattacarya, 1966, (Bhattacarya, 1966: 214). He simply states that 'a replacement in *yaṆ* in place of *iK* when *aC* follows' is seen in usage. It also means that Pāṇini is not the creator (karttā) of words. He only recalls (smarttā) them from usage.

Grammarians present the analysis of correct words by imagining (kalpanayā) their constituency in bases (prakṛti) and affixes (pratyaya) guided by the principle of *anvaya* 'concurrent presence' and vyatireka 'concurrent absence,' and by formulating general (utsarga), exception (apavāda) and residual (śeṣa) rules with related option (vibhāṣā), negation (pratiṣedha), restriction (niyama) and extension (atideśa), which, in turn, would capture usage by way of derivation (niṣpatti). Nāgeśa is quick to remind us that this analysis based on *kalpanā* 'imagination' has its validity only in the domain of grammar (śāstramātra-viṣayam). Since rules are formulated based on generalizations extracted from usage, and also since the scope of usage is very wide, a grammarian must find some standard norm of usage to facilitate determination of correctness. Patañjali states that the usage of the *śiṣṭa* 'wise, learned' should be accepted as the standard norm for usage. He identifies them as 'those brāhmaṇas who live in this home of the āryas, whose grain is only one little earthen pot, who are not greedy, who do not seize upon a cause and who, on account of something or the other, have gone to the end of some branch of learning, or other. This summary description of a *śiṣṭa* is based largely on *nivāsa* 'residence in Āryāvarta and ācāra 'conduct,' notions many would consider non-linguistic. One must remember here that ācāra and 'going to the end of one branch of learning' with on ulterior motive whatsoever, not only attest to their use of correct words but also affirms their excellence.

Grammarians accept that a word without meaning and a meaning without word does not exist. This makes śabda and artha inseparable. A word is that by means of whose articulation one properly comprehends its meaning. A word, in the outside world of usage, is accepted as sound which makes meaning comprehended. But since sound disappears quickly, and also since sound is simply the quality of word (śabda-guṇa), sound cannot only not be accepted as *nitya* 'eternal, permanent,' it cannot be accepted as that which expresses meaning. What expresses meaning is the the expressive power of word (śabda-śakti). The locus of this expressive power of word is sphoṭa 'that from which meaning bursts forth.' Identification of words within sentences, and of sounds with bases and affixes makes matters worse because meaning of a sentence, and for that matter of words, is not the sum total of meaning of their constituent units. Furthermore, a concurrent signification of meaning via experience of individual sound segments, and for that matter their combinations brought about by their sequential arrangement, cannot facilitate cognition of meaning. A disappearance of v from vṛkṣaḥ cannot account for the original meaning of vṛkṣaḥ A switch of *y, k, s* in *yūpaḥ sūpaḥ* and *kūpaḥ* may not be accepted as a significant variable in the denotation of meaning since it will render *ūpaḥ* vacuous. If one argues that recall of combinations will be made possible based on experience supported by memory, and hence, combinations of individual sound segments can be accepted as expressive, we will still face difficulties. For, saraḥ and rasaḥ, since they are composed with the same set of individual sound segments, may appear to denote the same meaning. For, memory will furnish an identical set of impression for sounds which compose these utterances. There is absolutely no one to one correspondence between formal units of sentences, their constituent words, and corresponding units of meaning. We, however, see that a whole is meaningful if its parts are also meaningful. Combinations are meaningful if individuals in combination are also meaningful. A whole of people with eyes is certainly capable of seeing things as the individual does. We also see that a whole does not denote any meaning if its parts do not. A single grain of sesame contains oil so also does a heap of sesame. But individual parts of a chariot do not posses gati 'movement' as the chariot does. Grammarians accept the *sphoṭa* of indivisible sentence (akhaṇḍa vakya-sphoṭa) as principal. Grammarians, at least for heuristic and analytic reasons, accept the sphota of component parts of sentences. In all practicality, the grammar of the three sages analyzes utterances of the Sanskrit language as an expression in sound of the word-on-mind (*buddhyārūḍha-śabda*) of the speaker guided by his intent to speak (vivakṣā). The domain of grammar encompasses infinite utterances of the language from dhvani to spohṭa. Study of meaning, and for that matter its cognition, falls outside of the scope of grammar. Grammar is limited to *lakṣya* 'usage' and *laksaṇa* 'rules.'

6

Notes on Kaṇva-Kṛṇva

Dipak Bhattacharya

1. Introductory

In 1940 Karl Hoffmann[1] (1940:148–161 = 1975:15–28) had suggested the derivation of the word *kaṇva* from the root *kṛ*- with thematisation of the present stem in the 5th *i.e.* the -nu- class. The view was opposed by F.B.J. Kuiper (1955 and 1991). The present paper aims at confirming the authenticity (which does not necessarily mean grammatical 'correctness' *i.e.* a regular grammatical derivation) of the form *kṛṇva* from three sources not noted by Hoffmann, namely, Pāṇini, the Dhātupāṭha and the Orissa manuscripts of the Paippalāda-Saṁhitā of the Atharvaveda discovered by Durgamohan Bhattacharyya[2] and attempting a critique of the controversy.

---

[1]Vedische Namen in Woerter und Sachen 21, 1940. Pp. 139–161. I consulted its reprint in Aufsaetze zur Indoiranistik, Band 1 and 2, Wiesbaden, 1875 ınd 1976. Ed. J. Narten, pp. 6–26

[2]Discovered in 1959 by Durgamohan Bhattacharyya. The first four kāndas edited by Bhattacharyya were published in two volumes by the Sanskrit College, Calcutta. in 1964 and 1970. See Bibliography. A new edition published by the Asiatic Society, Calcutta has since then appeared, Vol.1 kāṇḍas 1–15 (1997), Vol.2 kāṇḍa 16 (2008), Vol.3 kāṇḍas 17–18, (2011). The fourth volume (19–20) is with the press and is likely to come out soon.

The last evidence mentioned could not be available to Hoffmann in 1940. However, the Paippalāda occurrence has been brought to the notice of scholars since long, first by Durgamohan Bhattacharyya in the critical apparatus of the second volume of its edition by him (1970: p.262, n.8), by the present author[3] (1984) and by M. Witzel[4] (1997). But I do not know of any work on the first two evidences.

2. *Hoffmann's Views*

Hoffmann (*l.c*) systematically presented all the relevant information available at that time barring the one from the Dhātupāṭha and Pāṇini presented in this paper. He focused on the predominant occurrence of the word in the eighth maṇḍala of the Ṛgveda, the name Kaṇva in mythology, the meanings of the word, namely that of the mythical Kaṇva, of the sage Kaṇva and of one belonging to the family of Kaṇva; the adjectival use in the sense of 'deaf', 'praiser', 'one who is to be praised and lastly' 'evil'; syllabic anatomy of the word; etymology; evidence from Old Persian.

A gist of Hoffmann's arguments, spread over fourteen pages, is given below.

According to Hoffmann (22-) the retroflex -*ṇ*- in *kaṇva*, which is an invariable feature of the word since its earliest occurrence in the RV, could not be the result of spontaneous cerebralisation of dental -*n*- which was a general trend in MIA. The *ṇ* of *kaṇva* can only be explained as resulting from a preceding *r*- or *ṛ*. So one has to assume a basic form **kṛṇva* or **karṇva* from which *kaṇva* developed. Of the four possible resolutions of the basic forms – 1.**k-ṛṇva* -**k-arṇva*, 2**kṛ-ṇva* -**kar-ṇva*, 3**kṛṇ-va*-**karṇ-va*, 4**kṛṇv-a*- **karṇv-a* –1. the first one

---

[3]On the new material in the Atharvaveda Paippalāda *IIJ* 1984 173–188; p.183

[4]Cambridge 1997 257–345, para 2.5. Not available to me excepting in excerpts that I chanced to see. Witzel thinks that kṛṇva is a hypercorrect form made from the Ṛgvedic kaṇva. That does not take into account that it must, then, be assumed that the word existed as kaṇva with two meanings, one meaning the sage and the other evil doer. And that Pāṇini made kṛṇva from the one with the derogative meaning, perhaps to distinguish it from the name of the sage. But why should there be exactly the same word with two meanings? This would require a convincing explanation.

is absurd; 3.No root like *kr̥ṇ*, or *karṇ* exists which discards the third possibility which demands that *–va* is added to such a root. The third possibility, too, has to be discarded as it demands that *–va* has to be added to the root *kr̥ṇ* or *karṇ* while no such root exists 4. And the fourth resolution is 'insufficient'. For, it does not settle the issue as one shall still require the resolution of the first member. So (Hoffmann 23) one is left with the second possibility of **kr̥-ṇva-, kar-ṇva-*

In the second dissection the first part of the word can pertain to three Indo-Aryan roots – 1. *kr̥* to make, 2. *kr̥̄, kir* to scatter, 3. *kr̥* 'to commemorate', 'to praise'. Since *ṇva* is not known as a suffix it can only be a part of the verb. Now of the three verbs to be considered

√*kr̥* to commemorate has only one doubtful present form *cakrant*. Its other verbal and nominal derivatives have no bearing upon the form *kr̥(r̥)ṇva*. The same is true of for *kr̥̄*. As for *kr̥* 'to make' belonging to the *nu*-class, cf., *asunvá, hinvá, asinvá, dānupinvá* etc. The nominal forms with *nva* are, therefore, present-stem formations of the nu-class that is directly based upon the thematised present stem. *kr̥-ṇvá* is to be derived from √*kr̥* in the same manner. Of the two hypothetical basic forms **kar-ṇva* and **kr̥-ṇva*, the former's vowel gradation is not justified and hence is to be kept out of consideration.Káṇva and Kŕ̥ṇva corresponding to the R̥gvedic *hinvá* are, however, different in accent. But Káṇva is a proper name which shifts accent with adjective as in Kŕ̥ṣṇa 'proper name' but *kr̥ṣṇá* 'black', Rā́ma 'proper name' *rāmá* 'black'.

An evidence of the derivation of *kaṇva* from *kr̥* is the close connection of the word with Praskaṇva which takes this s after the preposition *sam, pari* (Ep.) and *upa*. One can summarise the results of the investigation as follows : The name *Káṇva* is a present-stem derivation of the root *kr̥* 'to make' and as its phonemic form is of dialectal origin. Kaṇva is a mythological figure and a forefather of the Kaṇva family to which the hymn-composers of the name of Kaṇva belong. But the word *kr̥'ṇva* (Note for editor: Please add accent marks to *r̥* DB) pertains to the sense of magical performance associated with √*kr̥*.

3. The word kaṇva *in the Orissa MSS of the AVP*

There are several verses in the AVP where the word *Kaṇva/Kaṇvā* appears as *Kṛṇva/Kṛṇvā* in the Or MSS and as *Kaṇva/Kaṇvā* in K. All the occurrences are described below.

The manuscripts have been described in the Critical apparatus of the 1997 edition. K is available for all the kāṇḍas but with frequent lacunae. The manuscripts available for the verses cited in this paper are as follows kāṇḍa 1 V, M_1,J_1; 4,5 V, M_1, M_2, J_1; 6-10,12 Mā, M_2; 19 Mā, M, J_2,J_3; 20 Mā, M,J_3. The sign + means reconstruction through comparison between K and Or. The manuscripts do not have accent marks.

3a. AVP 1.86.1–3 The Sanskrit text reproduced here is identical with the one in the critical edition as far as they are covered by the edited parts. A translation follows with variant readings and remarks where the occasional uncertain nature of the text has been noted with suggestions. The discussion concentrates on *kṛnva/kaṇva* and what appears to me to be the most important points; hence insignificant variants have not been necessarily cited. But they can be checked from the critical edition

1/1.86.1. *Tribhyo rudrebhyo pravasan yajāmi*
jyesṭhaḥ kanṣtha uta madhyamo yaḥ/
jyotiṣkārāḥ kavayaḥ somapā ye
kaṇvā adantu(<+*ajantu*) *nir ito vadhena*// 2.4.1610.22→↓

'To the three Rudras do I offer vaṣaṭ as prayāja, (he who is) the eldest, the youngest and who the middle one. The light-creating poets who are soma-drinkers may drive away the kaṇvas from here with a deadly weapon.'

Variants a K *pravasant yajāmi*; V, M *pravasajjajāmi* (V si →mi), J *pravaṣajjajāmi*; d Or *kṛṇvā, yajanti* and *ato*;

The hymn is exclusive to the AVP. There are three Or MSS and K. The entire hymn aims at ecorcising female evil spirits called kaṇva/ kaṇvā who are explicitly mentioned in the first three verses.

In the 1997 edition I noted that the reading in a had been retained from Bhattacharyya's 1964 edition in deference to the view of the late editor. Visibly it entails the deletion of the *t* of K and the replacement of its *ṣa* by *sa* occurring in two of the Or mss. The resulting meaning 'partant-en-voyage' (Renou 1964) is not inappropriate but so much change is not necessary. The translation implies *pra vaṣaḍ yajāmi* that involves only one change in J's *vaṣaj* and the adoption of K's *yajāmi*. This reading is supported by the fact that K's *-ḍya-* is close to its *–ntya-*. In *d* Or's *adantu* with *nir* hardly fits in. K's *yajanti* retains the original second consonant which, compared with Or, allows the reconstruction *nir ajantu* that the translation implies. Cf., 4.13.4 *nir-aja* 'drive away' below with Kaṇva as the object

2/1.86.2. *indrāgnī vītaṁ haviṣaḥ saṁvidānau samiddho agniḥ samidhā gīrbhir indraḥ/*
nudethāaṁ kaṇvā nir ito arātim ārād rakṣāṁsi tapataṁ vy asmat//

"O Indra and Agni! Enjoy the offering remaining in harmony. Agni has kindled the firewood, Indra the prayer. May you two drive away Kaṇvās, (drive) away from here the evil!"

3/1.86.3. *vāstoṣ pate suprajasaḥ suvīrā ṣaṣṭhīsyāmi* (*read* K *ṣaṣṭhyā* (*a*)*ṁśāni*) *śaradaḥ śatāni/*
durvāstu kaṇvā abhi nir ṇudasva suvāstu asmān upa saṁ viśasva//

O Lord of the house! With the sixth may I attain hundreds of autumns endowed with good progeny, with heroic sons! Push away the Kaṇvās to a bad house! Provide us with a good house!

Variants : b K *ṣaṣṭhyāṁśāni* Or's *ṣaṣṭhīsyāmi* 'I shall be the sixth' is unfit. K *ṣaṣṭhyāṁśāni* May I attain with the sixth' seems to refer to a sixth offering. The first verse speaks of three vaṣaṭs for three Rudras, the second invokes Indra and Agni obviously with prayers and offerings. *ṣaṣṭhyā* implies an understood *āhutyā*

One might give a thought also to *ṣaṣṭhyā* + *ānaśāni*, perf.subj,1/1 of *naś/aś* 'to attain' that involves conjectural emendation. *naś* should be from H*naś*, for the long *ā´* of *ānaśé/ānaṭ* (AVŚ 6.113.1,3/RV 7.7.7;AVŚ 18.3.65/ AVP 18.75.10) can be explained only as from H*a*H*naśe*/H*a*H*naṭ*, a verb beginning with a vowel being implausible (Kurylowicz *Études*

Indoeuropéennes:29 Krakow 1935). *ṣaṣṭhyā* + *naśāni*. Cf., Hoffmann 1976: 359,n.2 on *ā́naṭ.√naś* aor.subj.1/1. also is to be considered 12.4. 16 17.05/

AVP.4.13 = AVŚ 2.25 Where the text does not vary from that of the AVŚ Whitney's translation has been adopted. Four Or mss are available for the hymn. The current number of the verse is followed by its serial number beginning from 1.86 above

AVP.4.13

4/ 4.13.1 *śaṁ no devī pṛśniparṇī aśaṁ nirṛtaye karat/*
ugrā hi kaṇvajambhaṇī tāṁ tvāharṣaṁ sahasvatīm//

Weal for us, woe for Nirṛti has the divine spotted leaf made; since it is a formidable grinder up of *kaṇva* I fetched you as such, the powerful one.

Variants K *pṛṣṇyaparṇy...sahasvatī*/ Or...*pṛśniparṇnī śan... sarasvatīṁ*//

The AVŚ has *nírṛtyā akaḥ* and in d *tā"m abhakṣi* *

5/ 4.13.2 *sadānvāghnī prathamā pṛśniparṇy ajāyata/*
tayā kaṇvasyāhaṁ śiraś chinadmi śakuner iva//

'This spotted-leaf was first born as the killer of the sadānvās. By that do I cut off the head of the kaṇva as that of a bird.'

variants b K *pṛṣṇyaparṇy*../* *kaṇvasyam*...; c V * *kanvasyāhaṁ*...;
AVŚ has *sáhamāneyáṁ.../táyāháṁ durṇā'mṇāṁ śíro vṛścāmi...*//

6/ 4.13.3 *ūrjabhṛtaṁ prāṇabhṛtaṁ prajānām uta tarpaṇīm/*
sarvās tāḥ pṛśniparṇītaḥ kaṇvā mā anīnaśat//

Variants K * * * *upa* */ * *tvā pṛṣṇyaparṇī yataṣ kāṇvā anīśat/*

'Supporting strength, supporting life, also satisfying people, all those Kaṇvās did the spotted-leaf get me (?) make disappear from here.'

Explaining *mā in* Or's *mā anīnaśat* 'made me destroy (the kaṇvās)' in d, which is lacking in K, involves progressively complex sentences. One does not know if the mā is a later insertion or, if K has dropped a syllable as it often does. In both 3d and 7d K has dropped a syllable from the verb with √naś. The translation assumes a double causative in *anīnaśat*, the sense being 'made me drive away the Kaṇvās', the original verb *naś* being intransitive. The semantic substance of the three grades of *naś* vary in a progressive order –(1) *naś* 'to vanish' (intransitive *naśyati*), (2) *naś* (*nāś-i*) causative to get one disappeared *ie* make non-apparent or destroy one (transitive non-causative *nāśayati*) and (3) *naś* causative to make one get something vanished or destroyed (*nāśayati*). Ours is the third variety. It is not a common sentence type. The neat sense is that the *pṛśniparṇī* made me get the kaṇvās destroyed.

Theoretically, there is another possibility – that of *anīnaśat* being based on *naś/aṁś* to attain. But this seems unlikely to me.

I would have been happy to drop the *mā* that would have simplified the sentence and the work, but one has to be sure.

7/4.13.4 *samākṛtyainā nir aja tīkṣṇaśṛṅga iva ṛṣabhaḥ/*
arāyaṁ kaṇvaṁ pāpmānaṁ pṛśniparṇi sahasvati//

'Gathering these Kaṇvās together drive away like a sharp-horned bull the wizard Kaṇva, the sinful! O spotted leaf, the powerful one!'

Variants K *rāyaṁ kakaṇvaṁ* (dittography)*; Or * *kṛṇvaṁ**; exclusive AVP verse; first instance of a male *kṛṇva*; but he is in a group of females.

8/4.13.5 *tvam agre pṛśniparṇy*
agnir iva pradahann ihi kaṇvā jīvitayopanī/
girim enā ā veśaya
tamāṁsi yatra gacchāṁs tat pāpīr api pādaya//

'At the forefront do you, spotted-leaf, go like fire, burning the life obstructing *kaṇvās*! Make them enter the mountain where the darkness might go! There make you the sinners fall down!'

b V corrects *kaṇvā* to *kṛṇvā*. c K *jīvitayopinī*. Both Barret and Raghu Vira read *yopanī* while K has *yopinī*. Apparently both K and Or have lost the -ḥ of the plural ...*yopinīḥ* whose existence the translation assumes [Read .The translation assumes its existence.] c K *apa pātayaḥ*. The division of the pādas here is according to the Or MSS. It seems defective. Our a-c occur as AVŚ 2.25.4 in a different order and with variants. de occur there as vs 5cd [xxxdelted] with variants. The *kaṇvas* are male in the AVŚ.

9/4.13.6 *arāyam asṛkpāvānaṁ yaś ca sphātiṁ jihīrṣati/*
garbhādaṁ kaṇvaṁ nāśaya pṛśniparṇi sahasvati//

The blood-drinking wizard, who also wants to take away fatness, the embryo-eating kaṇva do thou make disappear, O spotted leaf, the overpowering one!

Or has *kṛṇvaṁ*. This is the third verse in the AVŚ.

10/4.13.7 *yā no gā yā no gṛhāṁ yā naḥ sphātim upāharān/*
tā ugre pṛśniparṇi tvaṁ kaṇvā mā nīnaśa itaḥ//

Who steal away our cows, who our houses, who our prosperity, them O mighty Spotted leaf, do thou make me get disappeared from here.

Variants cd K *ugre pṛśṇyaparṇis taṁ kaṇvā mā naśaitaḥ* z3z V...*mā anīnaśa itaḥ → nīnaśataḥ. J ...mā anīnaśa itaḥ.*

Exclusive AVP verse. *Kaṇvā* is in feminine gender. The form with *nīnaśa* in *d* is as in 4.13.3d above with the difference that while in 3d above there was a reduplicative causative aorist with preterite connotation, the unaugmented *nīnaśa*, adopted here on the authority of two Or manuscripts, is an instance of reduplicated aorist in causative injunctive form, without preterite connotation, a sense suggested by *nāśaya* of the previous verse.

11/ 7.11.7 *yas tvā patyuḥ pratirūpo jāro bhūtvā nipadyate/*
arāyaṁ kṛṇvaṁ pāpmānaṁ tam ito nāśayāmasi//

'He who having assumed the exact form of your husband, having become a paramour lies down with you, him the evil sinful kṛṇva do I make disappear from here.'

ab missing in K. c K *rāyaṁ kaṇvaṁ...*;

a and c are new but b and d occur as RV 10.162.5^{b} and 5^{d} which are, again, verbatim reproduced in AVŚ 20.96.15: *yás tvā́ bhrā́tā pátir bhūtvā́ jāró bhūtvā́ nipádyate/ prajā́ṁ yás te jíghāṁsatí tám itó nāśayāmasi//*

While editing the AVP when I reached kāṇḍa 7 I had become somewhat confident that *kaṇva* is an archaic form. Hence I adopted the Or reading in the text.

Apart from K there are only two Or manuscripts for AVP 6-15.

12/12.7.1 (Barret and Raghu Vira 13.4.1)=AVŚ 4.37.1
tvayā pūrvam atharvāṇo jaghnū rakṣāṁsy oṣadhe/
tvayā jaghāna kaśyapas tvayā kṛṇvo agastyaḥ//

'By thee of old did the Atharvans slay the demons, O herb, by thee did Kaśyapa slay, by thee Agastya, the *kṛṇva*.'

Variants b K jaghano d K kaṇvo →M2 c up to kṛ mutilated

AVŚ 4.37.1 *káṇvo*. Whitney takes *káṇvo* as proper noun meaning the sage of that name, but the adjectival character of the word, qualifying Agastya is more plausible.

13/ AVP 12.20.2 (Barret and Raghu Vira 13.10.4)
Ya ārebhe yasya vā ghāsy apsarā yaḥ kṛṇvena saṁvido yātumāvān/
ulūkayātuṁ bhṛmalo yasya yātus tam [atrāpi pra daha jātavedaḥ

He who seizes, for whom you are indeed unenjoyable (apsarā), who, the sorcerous, gets united (saṁvide K) with the *kṛṇva*, the owl-sorcerer,whose sorcery is the black-bee,(?bhṛmalo), him do thou burn here, O Jātavedas

Variants a K *ārebhe sya... yuṣ kaṇvena saṁvide yātumāvāṁ ulūkayātu bhramalo yasya yātus tvaṁ;*

Exclusive AVP verse

saṁvido of Or looks unacceptable.

14/ AVP 20.56.7 (K 20.52.7)
roce mā prakāśe mā kṛṇvāvidaṁ mā gamaya/ anu mā budhyantām//

'Me to radiance, me to light, me the knower of kṛṇva do thou lead! Let (others) awaken after me.'

Variants : K b *kaṇvāvidaṁ * gamayaḥ*; c *Mā budhyatāṁ*// K *vudhnyantām*

Exclusive AVP verse and, but for one verse (vs.8), also excusive AVP hymn. 4.5.1613.19The hymn aims at violent magic. *kṛṇva* seems to be action noun meaning magical act.

Of *kṛṇva/kaṇva* we got nine ṛ-forms, all occurring in Or and five a-forms. There are five more doubtful ṛ-forms that are being discussed below.

15/6.20.6/= AVŚ 19.47.6[abc]; a=RV 6.71.3[d], 6.75.10[d],(AVP 15.10.10[d])
rakṣā mā kṛṇvo aghaśaṁsa īśata/mā no duḥśaṁsa īśata//

K * *mākirṇo* * *.../ AVŚ *rákṣā mā́kir ṇo aghá́śaṁsa ī́śata mā́ no duḥśáṁsa ī́śata*// /RV *rákṣā mā́kir ṇo aghá́śaṁsa ī́śata*//

It is not difficult, perhaps too easy, to emend the MS readings *mā kṛṇvo* (Or) or *mākir ṇo* (K) to *mākir no* in the AVP so that the translation 'Protect, let no mischief-plotter have mastery over us!'. But the uniform occurrence of –ṇ- in K and Or i.e. in all the three mss available for the AVP is an impediment.

rakṣā (*rákṣā* AVŚ and RV) is an independent sentence connected to the subsequent part of the verse narratively but not syntactically. We inferred a *naḥ* 'us'.

16/ 8.2.8=AVŚ 5.13.9
karṇā śvāvid abravīd girer avacarantikā/
yāḥ kāś cemāḥ khanitrimās tāsām arasatamaṁ viṣam//
K *kaṇvā * * gired * * * yemā khanitrimās * arama.../*

'The eared hedgehog said this, coming down from the mountain; whichsoever of these (f) are produced by digging, of them the poison is most sapless.' (Whitney)

AVŚ has an extra *tád* before *abravīd*, otherwise the Or reading tallies with it.

karṇā́ 'stutzohrig' – Wackernagel-Debrunner AiG 2.2 :137-138.

Apparently, there is a corruption of *karṇā* in K that reads *kaṇvā* for *karṇā*. But it appears that there are only two instances (see below for the other one) of *karṇā/-a* being read *kaṇvā/-a* in K. In both cases the word fits into the context as an adjective. Note that there are nine instances of Or's *kṛṇva* being read as *kaṇva* in K but none of Or's *karṇa* being read as *kaṇva* excepting these two.

17/ 9.10.6
paruṣas tvāmṛtakarṇo viṣa prathamam āvayat+/ yathā ha taṁ nāropayas tathāsy arasaṁ viṣam//
'Puruṣa, producing immortality, first consumed (?) you, O poison! That you do not afflict him so are you sapless'.
Variants: K *puruṣas* (adopted) ...*kaṇvo* * * *āvayam*/ * *tanvāropayas*.../ Or...*āmayat*/

Remarks: Exclusive AVP verse. The second quarter occurs also as 5.8.2^{b}. The translation assumes the emendation *tvāmṛakṛṇva* with –*kṛṇva* irregularly formed from the present tense stem *kṛṇv-*. The first pāda then stands as *puruṣas tvā 'mṛtakṛṇvo*. For the *amṛta* connection of Puruṣa also cf., 9.5.4^{cd} *utāmṛtasyeśvaro yad annenābhavat saha*/
This speaks for our rejection of the Or reading *paruṣa*

18/19.7.5 =AVŚ 6.52.3
āyurvidaṁ vipaścitaṁ śrutāṁ +kaṇvasya vīrudham/
āhārṣaṁ viśvabheṣajīm asyādṛṣṭāṁ ni śamaya//
Securing (a long) span of life, the inspired, famous plant of *Kaṇva*, I gathered (that) healer of all; pacify his unseen ones!
Variants: b K karṇasya

AVŚ 6.52.3
āyurdadaṁ vipaścitaṁ śrutāṁ kaṇvasya vīrudham/
ābhārịṣaṁ viśvabheṣajīṁ asyādhṭān ni śamayat//

'The life(*ā́yus*)-giving'inspired (*vipaścít*), famous plant of *Kaṇva*, the all-healing one, have I brought; may it quench this man's unseen ones.' (Whitney) This is practically identical with my translation.

19/19.28.10
ā no medhā sumatir viśvarūpā giro bṛhatīr āveśayantī/
ṛco me bahvī ny anaktu gā iva yathāsāma bhuvaneṣu kaṇvinaḥ//
'May our intelligence, well-intentioned, having all forms, infusing great songs (into me), anoint many of my verses like cows so that we may be *kaṇvins* among beings'.

Variants: K ****sumatis supratīkā śiror bṛhaspatīkā giror bṛhaspatir */ruco *bahvīn niyunaktu *va ...*; Or d ...*karṇṇanaḥ//* (p.15 orig paper ends)

Excl AVP vs. The translation implies the emendation *bahvīr* in c. The word at the end should be either *karṇiṇaḥ* or *kaṇvinaḥ* as in K or *kṛṇvinaḥ* if our view about the original word were correct. *karṇinaḥ* 'possessed of ears' meaning 'attentive listeners' should not be inappropriate.

Till now we got nineteen cases of *kṛṇva/kaṇva* including five doubtful cases, all of which barring one, (no.18 AVP19.7.5/18 =AVŚ 6.52.3) [AVŚ 6.52.3 *āyurdadaṁ vipaścitaṁ śrutāṁ kaṇvasya vīrudham/ ābhāriṣaṁ viśvabheṣajīṁ asyādhṭān ni śamayat//*] concerns some activity of *kaṇva* of some evil or violent type. No 18 addresses the herb of *kaṇva*. It may mean some antidote. Hence the appeal is for quenching the 'unseen' of *Kaṇva ie* warding off the effect of unforeseen acts (*adṛṣṭān*) of *Kaṇva*.

There are five further occurrences in the same sense, all in feminine gender and in exclusive AVP verses. Though none of them have the *-ṛ-* element, the verses are discussed below in order to arrive at the prevalent sense of the word in the AVP.

20/ 5.9.3 Hymn against *sadānvās, kaṇvās* etc.
sahaḥ sahaḥsaty (read *sahasvaty*) *asītaḥ kaṇvāḥ paro 'nudat/*
imā yā adhunā gatā yāś ceha grahaṇīḥ purā//

Variants: K *māsahāsaty amīdas kāṇvā * nudaḥ/ mā * dhanā ** ciha gṛṇīṣ puraḥ/*
The mss do not have the apostrophe in b *'nudat/nudaḥ.*
'Powerful, full of strength you are, you drove away (read *nudaḥ*) the kaṇvās from here, those who went now, and also those who were seizing formerly.'

21/ AVP 5.9.5
viteru panthāḥ śvaśre bibhide te gadohanī/dadhau te adya gauṣ kaṇve parehy avaraṁ mṛṇe//
K *vitenmanthā ścaśire vitade * agadohinī dadau * abhya * kaṇve * * vṛṇe/*

'Your churner immediately fell apart, your club-mover split apart, your cow was burnt(?) today, O *Kaṇvā*, go far away down, you crusher.'

The translation is based upon the reading *vi te *nu manthāḥ śaśrire bibhide* etc. In c read *dadau*, after K, from √du 'to be burnt'. Note in d *mṛṇe* = voc/1 of *mṛṇā* the unprefixed feminine stem. The formation of the nominal *mṛṇa* should be from √*mṛ* : AiG 2.2: 726.

22/ 10.1.8
kaṇvā yā gardabhīva nibhasat sūkarīva/tasyai prati pra vartaya taptam aśmānam āsani//

'*Kaṇvā* who is like an ass, (who) devours like a swine, for her put back in the mouth a hot stone.' The translation is literal; it is implied that *Kaṇvā* resembles an ass also in devouring. *prati pravartaya* should imply counter-witchcraft but that one misses in the context.

23,24/. 19.36.15,16.
AVP 19.36.15 *indreṇa dattaṁ balam āsurābhyāṁ śita*(<ā?)*ṁguitac chālvatāyai ca tubhyam/ tau nudethāṁ kaṇvā aśivā* 10.51/ 15.49 *ajuṣṭā adhā gṛhāṇāṁ gṛhapā stam esām//*

19.3616 *tvam agne gṛhapatir gṛhāṇāṁ tvaṁ prajānāṁ janitāsi dātā/*
tvaṁ nudasva kaṇvā aśivā ajuṣṭāḥ sadānvā nir ataḥ seda pāpīḥ//

'Strength was given by Indra to the two Āsuras, O Śitaṁga, this to you and also to Śālvatā(?). As such you two may drive away the Kaṇvās, the inauspicious and unpropitious ones. Then you remain the lord of their houses!' 15

'O Agni, you are the lord of the houses, you are the begetter, the donor of progeny. You drive away the inauspicious and unpropitious Kaṇvās, the Sadānvās do you drive away from here, the sinful ones.'

Variants K * * * *āsurabhyāṁ śṛṁgaituś chālvatāye* * * *taṁ nudasva* * *śivaṁjuṣṭā padānvā nidadhasyeda pāpī*/

Mā ...rābhya śi→sita chālvai ca */...asivā ayuyuṣṭā***stum* *//*asivā yuyṣṭā* * * *ajaḥ* * *pāpīṁ*//

J_2 has *āśivā* in both the verses; J_3...*ccākvatāyai...asivā ayuṣṭā*...//...*gṛhapati* * * *... * si */* *nudasya* * *ajivā yuṣṭāḥ sadānya* * *itaḥ* * *pāpīṁ*//

M has *nir itaḥ* in d/

Apart from the above ones there are seven instances where the sage *Kaṇva* has been mentioned. They are 2.14.5 (AVŚ 2.32.3),4.38.4(AVŚ 4.29.5), 5.25.2 (AVŚ 4.19.2), 6.17.11 (RV 1.14.2), 8.15.2 (*agastyaḥ kaṇvāḥ kutsāḥ*), 11.2.6 (*tayā bharadvājaḥ kaṇvo*) and 20.4.4 (AVŚ 7.15.1)

4. The meaning of kṛṇva/kaṇva

We have mentioned twentyfour cases. Of them nine have the form *kṛṇva*, ten have *kaṇva* and five are doubtful cases.

Among the doubtful cases 6.20.6 (no.15 above) has *mā kṛṇvo* in Or and *mākir ṇo* in K which occurs as AVŚ 19.47.6 and also at many other places including RV 6.71.3). Or's *mā kṛṇvo* and K's *mākir ṇo* both yield meaning but since *mākir* is a familiar word and occurs as such in the parallel stanzas it might be preferred by scholars unless they are keen on the relevance of the *mā kṛṇvo* reading.

Also 8.2.8 (no.16) has *karṇā* in Or that is identical with the AVŚ (5.13.9) reading. 19.7.5 (no.18 K *karṇasya*, Or *karṇaśca*) has *kaṇvasya* in its parallel AVŚ version and most probably refers to the sage *Kaṇva*. The three are kept out of consideration though their acceptance as *kṛṇva* forms would have strengthened our case. But the two other doubtful cases - 9.10.6 (no.17) and 19.28.10 (no.19) cannot be easily disposed of. So we have to discuss 19+2 that is twentyone cases.

They are a kind of evil beings. *Kṛṇva* is a present stem derivative. This is important. The unusual morphology *ie* not forming a nominal by adding a suffix to the root *kṛ* serves the purpose of conferring a special sense to the derivative and thereby distinguishing it also semantically from *kara* the usual thematic derivative of *kṛ*. We shall see that the special sense could only be that of evil or violence.

The evil activities of *Kaṇva* are indicated in AVP 4.13.5: 'life-obstructing'(5), 'blood-drinking', 'fat-stealing', and 'embryo-eating'(6) and 'sinful' (*passim*). This is also true of 7.11.7 and 12.20.2. The subject matter of 12.20.2 involves magical activity of the violent type. 'He who seizes, who, the sorcerous, gets united with kṛṇva, the owl sorcerer, whose sorcery is the black-bee...' They cause seizure, (*grahaṇīḥ*) 5.9.3, have churners and medicine-gathering implements (*agadohanī* 5.9.5). In 12.7.1 *kṛṇva* is an adjective qualifying Agastya, the reputed sage of the Purāṇas, but the reference is to Agastya's action as the slayer of the demons. That means the name *kṛṇva's* connection with violent activity exists here too.

Magical action attaches to the word *kṛṇva-* in *kṛṇvāvidam* 'the knower of *kṛṇva*' of 20.56.7 too.

There may be statistical variation on account of the marginally unhappy state of the text but there cannot be any doubt that one line of development of the word *kaṇva/kṛṇva* was in the sense of magical action of the violent type. All the nine *kṛṇva* forms belong to this type - three are nouns in the feminine gender, four are such in masculine, one is a masculine adjective and one is an action noun. The thematic -a- form occurs eight times in the feminine gender and twice in the masculine.

The prevalence of the sense of action, adjectival use and the evil connection point to the possibility of the derivation of the word from kṛ in the sense which made the development of the word *kṛtyā* 'sorcery' (cf., AVP 16.35.5 *kṛtyāḥ santu kṛtyākṛte*; AVŚ 4.9.5 *na kṛtyā nābhiśocanam* etc; also see AiG 2.2, p.832 §665c) from the same root possible. However, this is only a possibility that cannot be strongly insisted upon. In fact, most probably, *kṛtyā* has its origin in the ancient verb *kṛntati* 'cuts'; cf., *kərəmtāt̰* Vend.7.37 Bartholomae 'schneiden' also cf., Beng. *kā̃ā̃ṭā*< Sans. *kaṇṭaka*, 'thorn'< **kṛntaka*). In that case the loss of *-n-* in *kṛtyā*, however, has to be accounted for.

The *kṛṇva* form, if it is authentic, was retained only in one tradition transmitted through the Or MSS varied with the more prevalent *kaṇva* form. The sage, however, is invariably mentioned as Kaṇva. Of eighty such occurrences the K variant *karṇasya* in 19.7.5 does not seem to be significant of the existence of the -ṛ- form in this sense.

The word *kaṇva* is incidentally mentioned by the Vārtikakāra on P 3.1.14 (*kaṣṭāya kramaṇe*). The vārtika runs *satra-kakṣa-kaṣṭa-kṛcchra-gahanebhyaḥ kaṇvacikīrṣāyām*. Patañjali paraphrases by repeating the vārtika and adding *iti vaktavyam*. One sees that *kaṇva* is not the object word in the vārtika. That means the Vārtikakāra assumes that the meaning of the word *kaṇva* should be wellknown. It is Kaiyaṭa who paraphrases in the commentary Pradīpa *satrādayo'tra vṛttiviṣaye pāpaparyāyāḥ*. Then he further clarifies by explaining the word *kaṇva* occurring in the vārtika - *kaṇvaṁ pāpam ucyate*. Nāgeśa adds in his commentary Udyota *pāpacikīrṣāyāṃ gamyamānāyām ity arthaḥ* The net result is that according to Kaiyaṭa and Nāgeśa *kaṇva* means 'evil'

5 The position of Pāṇini

5a. Introductory

The form *kṛṇva* has not been noted in our commentarial literature on the Vedas or on Pāṇini. But the sense of 'evil' or 'sin' has not gone unnoticed in grammatical literatue literature.

The word *káṇva* occurring in Uṇādisūtra √149[5] meaning pāpam (below), has been meant as derived from the root *kaṇ* in the said

---

[5]A. No 149 in √*Vaiyākaraṇasiddhāntakaumudī* ed. Giridharisarma Chaturvedi MLBD Delhi 1961, p.153;√ B. no.157 √ in Pandit Harishankara Pandeya's edition Patna 1938 as per A.P.Banerji-Sastri's Foreword; page no. occurs separately for each section); √C. Sūtra 4351 (=1.153) in Bombay Khemaraj Krishnadas 1929 edition, p.604;√D.152 in S.C.Vasu's 1907,Allahabad edition: p.184. A critical edition of the Uṇādisūtras is a desideratum.

sūtra, and, according to Bhaṭṭoji Dīkṣita, as meaning *pāpam* (evil) in his notes to the above mentioned uṇādisutra that runs as follows *aśū-pruṣi-laṭi-kaṇi-khaṭi-viśibhyaḥ kvan*. 'To the roots *aś, pruṣ, laṭ, kaṇ, khaṭ* and *viś* is added the suffix (*k*)*va*(*n*).' The word *kaṇva* itself is not mentioned in the sutra. The root *kaṇ*(*i*)- and the suffix –(*k*) *va*(*n*) occur in the sutra and the word *kaṇva* has been meant to be inferred from the rule in a regular process. The operative part of the suffix *kvan* is *va*. That means one should add that *va* to the root *kaṇ*. Bhaṭṭojī Dīkṣita[6] mentions the meaning of *kaṇva* by adding the note *kaṇvaṁ pāpam bāhulakād kiṇvam api* "*kaṇva* means 'evil' 'sin'; since it is enjoined at random (*bāhulakād*) one also gets *kiṇvam*"

Before Bhaṭṭojī Dīkṣita the commentators on Patañjali's Mahābhāṣya explained *kaṇva* occurring the word kaṇvacikitsā in Vartika 1 on P 3.1.14 (*dhinvikṛṇvyor a ca*) as *pāpam* 'sin', 'evil'.

5b The forms kaṇva *and* kṛṇva

The form of the word which has been transmitted down to us through post-Pāṇinian literature is always *kaṇva*. But there are traces of the other form *kṛṇva*, which as we have seen occurs in the AVP.

For example, the sutra P. 3.1.80 *dhinvi-kṛṇvyor a ca* (below) might make one think that while composing this sūtra Pāṇini had the form *kṛṇva* in mind just as the author of the Dhātupāṭha had while recording the roots √*kṛṇv* and √*dhinv* in the *bhū* class.

The matter is being clarified below.

P.3.1.80 *dhinvi-kṛṇvyor a ca* means 'The roots √*dhinv*- and √*kṛṇv*- shall have the suffix -*a*- before -*u*-' instead of (*ś*)a(*p*) *ie* in the present conjugation, for *śap* is a stem suffix for the present conjugation.

According to Kāśikā this refers to the roots *dhivi* and *kṛvi* read as Dhātupāṭha I.593 and I.598.[...dhivi(DP 593) prīṇanārthā,...kṛvi hiṁsākaraṇayoḥ (DP 598)] √ One has to note that the roots are read in the bhū-class. The meaning entries which were added later

---

[6]See n.2. *Vaiyākaraṇasiddhāntakaumudī* ed. Giridharisarma Chaturvedi MLBD 1961, p.153)(p21,para 4).

according to tradition[7] record 'to please' for the former and 'to injure, to do' and also 'to move' according to Bhaṭṭoji Dīkṣita for the latter.

The above two roots had been entered into the Dhātupāṭha definitely before Pāṇini because, as the following discussion might show, the sutra would not have been necessary if these two roots had not been read in the bhū-class in the Dhātupāṭha before Pāṇini.

The bhū-class forms the present stem with an unaccented strengthening *a* that guṇates the weak vowel of the verb as in *bhū śap ti → bhávati*. √*dhinv* and √*kṛṇv* occur in a series of twelve roots in the Dhātupāṭha all ending in –nv. The roots occur serially as 587-598 with dhinv at no.593 and kṛṇv at no 598 . The meaning 'to please' (dhivi... prīṇanārthāḥ) is stated for dhinv and to injure and to move for kṛvi

The roots are presented in the Dhātupāṭha as dhivi and kṛvi. The metalinguistic presentation will be unintelligible without some explanation. The *i* of the roots is indicatory of the insertion of *n*- after the final vowel of the root by *idito num dhātoḥ* (P.7.1.58) which leaves the actual roots as √dhinv and √kṛṇv. The final *i*'s in the sutra itself are for the sake of pronunciation.

They form a-ending conjugational stems (P.3.1.68) like*'inva, jínva, ráṇva, hínva* etc.

The prescription of the sutra under discussion (3.1.80) has not been necessary for them. The sutra aims at making the present conjugation of √*kṛ* and √*dhi* like that of the verbs of the nu-class i.e. the fifth class. The process is as follows.

The roots are presented in the Dhātupāṭha as *dhivi* [*bhū*-class 593] and *kṛvi* [(*bhū*-class 598]. The –*i* is indicatory of the instruction to insert an –*n*– after the final vowel of the root (P. 7.1.58) which leaves

---

[7]That the meaning entries in the Dhātupāṭha are not original to it has been noted by Vāsudeva Dīkṣita in his commentary on the additional notes of Bhaṭṭoji Dīkṣita trailing the quoted verse *saṁhitaika* pade *nityā etc* (*pp.53-54 MLBD edn Vol.3*). *Vāsudeva states on the supposed authority of Patañjali* (*ibid p.54*)*: Pāṇinir hi dhātupāṭhe dhātūn kāṁś cid arthasahitān kāṁś cid artharahitān paṭhatīti cuṭū sūtrabhāṣye sthitam*. But I did not find the said discussion on the meaning of *dhātus* in the Mbh on *cuṭū* P.1.3.7 (p.209-211, Haryana edn). This perhaps is inferred from the utterance *yad ayam iritaḥ kāṁś cin num-anuṣaktān paṭhati 'ubundir niśamane' 'skandir gatiśoṣaṇayor'*.

the actual roots as √*dhinv* and √*kṛṇv*. The final –*i*'s in the sutra itself [after *dhinv* and *kṛṇv*] are for the sake of pronunciation. Patañjali (below) has taken care that no confusion took place on this.

Pāṇini[3.1.80] enjoins the substitution of the final consonant of the two roots [*dhinv* (*dhivi* Dp 593...) and *kṛṇv* (*kṛvi* Dp598...)] *i.e.* of –*v* by –a [that is to be]followed by u. instead of adding the normal (ś)a(p) i.e. the unaccented strong a (P.3.1.68 *kartari śap*). The –u– enjoined in 3.1.80 mentioned above follows from the previous sutra ie from 3.1.79. The stems thus formed are kṛṇ-a-u and dhin-a-u. In 3/1 the generated steps are kṛṇ-a-u-ti and dhin-a-u-ti. The a- is then elided by P. 6.4.48 [*ato lopaḥ*] generating kṛṇuti and dhinuti. Since the terminal suffix –ti[p] is not weak(enintg) (P.1.2.4) [*sārvadhātukam apit*] the preceding -u- is guṇated by P.7.3.84 [*sārvadhātukārdhdhātukayoḥ*] resulting in the forms *kṛṇoti* and *dhinoti.*

The dual and plural terminations –tas and –anti are weak (P. 1.2.4) in the sense that they do not strengthen the previous vowel. So forms like *kṛṇutas* and *kṛṇvanti* are possible.

The cumbrous process has been partly explained by Patañjali. He explains the necessity of postulating the additional –a– which is eventually elided. Without this, he explains, we would have got the *-u-* directly after dhin- and kṛṇ and by P 7.3.36 [*puganta laghūpadhasya ca*] the penultimate vowels *-i-* and *-ṛ-* would have to be guṇated [to *e* and *ar*]. The -a- is elided but its effect remains by P.1.1.57 (*acaḥ parasmin pūrvavidhau*) so that so that [notionally] the *-u-* does not come directly after *dhin* and *kṛṇ* and cannot effect guṇation as the vowels *-i-* and *-ṛ-* cannot be viewed as penultimate because of the intervention of the notional *-a-*.

But another question has not been raised by Patañjali. The root √*kṛ* is also read in the *-nu-* class that is the 5th conjugation (no.1253) with *-nu-* present stem-suffix and means 'to injure' [*kṛñ hiṁsāyām*] according to the meaning entry. In active present conjugation it has no difference from the forms of the root *kṛṇv-* of the *bhū*-class. The process is much simpler too. By 5.6.16 one has to add the stem-suffix *nu* to the root. The stem-suffix *nu* (3.1.73), is itself weak *i.e.* it does not strengthen the preceding vowel of the root. 3/1 –ti being strong ie capable of effecting guṇation on the preceding vowel (P.1.2.4) effects guṇation in nu. So we get the form *kṛṇoti*. Similarly, for reasons already stated *kṛṇutaḥ* and other present forms also are possible in the nu-class. [Hence] (read instaed)Now rises the question what is then the necessity of reading the root kṛ additionally as kṛṇv in the bhū-class?

With √dhi[nv] the question is a bit different. It (*dhinoti*) does not belong to the *nu*-class. But had it been included there we would have got the same forms as prescribed for √*dhinv* in the bhū-class. So, one may ask [about] the reason for its inclusion as √*dhinv* in the bhū-class instead of as √*dhi* in the nu-class.

It should be clear that the circuitous process described above has been necessitated by the inclusion of the roots in the *bhū*-class of the Dhātupāṭha. Without the sutra the normal course of the *bhū*-class would have given forms like *dhinvati* and *kṛṇvati* which Pāṇini wants to avoid. But without such inclusion in the Dhātupāṭha the cumbersome sūtra would have been superfluous.

As to the question why the roots were then at all included in the *bhū*-class, the way to arrive at the answer should be evident.

The sūtra pertains only to the present conjugation. That means the circuitous process is necessary only for the present conjugation. Since the process is circuitous for the present conjugation by the rule of inverse variation the inclusion of the sūtra in the *bhū*-class must have simplified the procedure for some non-present stem-formation, namely, non-present conjugational stem or non-conjugational i.e. nominal stem formation.

As to the exact form whose procedure is actually simplified, with √*dhi* the solution has been shown by Vāsudevadīkṣita in the Bālamanoramā commentary on the Siddhānta-Kaumudī. He illustrates our sūtra with *adhinvīt,* an *iṣ*-aorist ind. form, among others. This is found in the Pañcaviṁśa-Brāhmaṇa 4.10.1 With √*dhi* in the *nu*-class the vikaraṇa *nu,* that is the present-tense stem suffix, would have to be substituted by other appropriate suffixes (P.3.1.43) in the aorist conjugation making the form *adhinvīt* possible. That would not have been possible with √*dhi* in the *nu* class.25, para 2.

But no non-present conjugation with the nu-class is known for the root √*kṛ* in the in the nu-class. Then how was the form *kṛṇva* arrived at? We are forced to consider the possibility of the *kṛṇu*-stem being used for the formation of a nominal stem necessitating the recognition of the root √*kṛṇv* by the author of the Dhātupāṭha. **kṛṇva* is such a nominal stem. Hence its existence when the root √*kṛṇv* was included in the Dhātupāṭha has to be inferred.

One more point needs clarification. While √*dhinv* is found only in the *bhū*-class √*kṛṇva* is so read in addition to √*kṛ* in the in the nu-class. This double treatment is caused by the absence of the nu-stem for √*kṛ* for its non-present conjugation in contrast to its invariable presence with √*dhi*, that supposes the root as dhinv (**dhivi*) in conjugation. Thus we have cakāra (prf), akarat (a-aorist) etc from kṛ in non-present conjugation. There is no sign of the nu element here which persists in the present stem. But dhi is always with the nu. Cf., Visva Bandhu's *Padānukramakoṣa* that does not record any form derived from the root √*dhi* without the *nu*-element. That means it was part of the root but not a stem-forming morpheme. Hence its inclusion in the *nu*-class was unnecessary that is to say √*dhinv* itself served every purpose. In contrast the root *kṛ* has got a second additional characteristic in that it has both parasmaipada (active) and ātmanepada (middle) conjugation. The other ten roots read in the Dhātupāṭha along with √*dhinv*- and √*kṛṇv* are all conjugated exclusively in the parasmaipada (active). Both these differences of √kṛ from √dhi required the recognition of a separate root in the *nu*-class.

However, theoretically *dhinv* and *kṛṇv* may generate forms like *didhinva* and *cakṛṇva*. These are not attested, nor is there any possibility of finding them if the author of the *Dhātupāṭha* had only *adhinvīt* and *kṛṇva* in his mind. How Pāṇini looked at this matter is not known to me. Whitney (*The roots, verb-forms and primary derivatives of the Sanskrit language*, New haven, 1885 rep. Delhi 1963) records *didhinva* as one of the verb-forms under √*dhi, dhinv*' (p.83) and remarks (Preface, p.vii) "Of the verb-forms which, though not yet found ... in recorded use, are prescribed or authorized by Hindu grammarians, a liberal presentation is made under the different roots...'. He does not make any such 'liberal presentation' of *kṛ*-verb forms. However, at least two Indian grammarians (see below) spoke of such theoretical forms.

6 Post-Pāṇinian grammarians

No early grammarian raises the question of the necessity of accepting the roots √*kṛṇv* and √*dhinv*. This is in striking contrast to some vigorous discussion of some meta-linguistic problem with P.3.1.80.

Patañjali, for example, asks the necessity of replacing the –v of the root by –a and then eliding it instead of instead of mentioning it as a straight away elision. This has already been discussed.

The other point raised is the necessity of reading the roots as *dhinvi* and *kṛṇvi* instead in the usual mode of reading *i.e.* as *dhivi* and *kṛvi*. He does not defend Pāṇini. After some metalinguistic arguments he concludes: *tasmād dhivikṛvyor iti vaktavyam* 'So one should have read *dhivi* and *kṛvi*'.

The following works, among many others, do not go beyond the points raised by Patañjali: Kāśikā, Kāśikāvivaraṇapañjikā of Jinendrabuddhi (8th century), Kaiyaṭa's Pradīpa on the Mahābhāṣya (10th cent.?), Haradatta's Padamañjarī (10th cent.?) on the Kāśikā, Bhāṣāvṛtti of Puruṣottamadeva (12th cent.), Bhaṭṭoji Dīkṣita's Śabdakaustubha (Ed. Gopal Śāstrī Nene, Varanasi 1919).

Maitreyarakṣita (c.1100) records *cakṛṇva* in his Dhātupradīpa (ed. with annotations Srish Chandra Chakravarti, Rajshahi, 1919] under bhū 598, p. 44 without comments. His own words are *kṛvihiṁsākaraṇayoḥ kṛṇoti, cakṛṇva*. According to my knowledge the form is not attested]. The Tattvabodhinī (17th cent.) by Jñanendra Sarasvatī on the Siddhāntakaumudī of Bhaṭṭoji Dīkṣita comes near the problem but does not go into it: '... in the parasmaipada with sārvadhātuka endings (i.e. in the present tense D.B.) forms like *kṛṇoti* etc. would be the same for both (√ kṛṇv and √kṛ).' (Tattvabodhinī on SK 2332 = P. 3.1.80). The partial superfluity of the inclusion of the root √kṛ in the nu-class is noted but the very necessity of including it in the *bhū*-class is not discussed. [Jñānendrasarasvatī's own words are '*parasmaipadeṣu sārvadhātuke kṛṇotītyādīni rūpāṇi tulyānīti phalito 'rthaḥ*' (MLBD Vol.3 1965-2011: 157)

As noted above Maitreyarakṣita (Maitreya Rakṣita in orig paper) just mentions *cakṛṇva*. Viśveśvara Sūri (Vyākaraṇasiddhāntasudhānidhi Part 1, Chap.1-3, ed. Satyaprakash Dube, Pub. Rajasthan Patrika, Jodhpur, 1995), most probably belonging to the early eighteenth century, discusses the form for the first time in Vyākaraṇasiddhāntasudhānidhi, a commentary on the Aṣṭādhyāyī. He adds to his commentary on 3.1.80:

> "The following is to be noted here. We get the root kṛ in the sense of injuring in the nu-class. Forms like *kṛṇoti* etc. are the same for √*kṛṇv* and √*kṛ*. In the ātmanepada one gets forms like *kṛṇute* etc. (in the *nu*-class). In perfect one gets forms like *cakāra* in the *nu*-class) just as it is in the u-class. (i.e. eighth conjugation). With these two roots one gets *cakṛṇva* etc."

The actual occurrence of the stem *kṛṇva* in a particular sense in the Or MSS of the AV Paippalāda indicates that the solution lies not in (Read: illustration should not be) the hypothetical *cakṛṇva* but in the existence of (delete 'in the existence 'Read 'the nominal stem kṛṇva'). The word had become almost (del 'almost') long ago. That explains the hypothesisation and groping in darkness of the grammarians about √*kṛṇv*.

One may ask about the time when the form became obsolete. There is nothing to prove that *kṛṇva* and *dhinva* had been common stems in use. But, if our findings were correct, then the author of the Dhātupāṭha did know the conjugational stem *dhinv* most probably from the Pañcaviṁśa Brāhmaṇa 4.10.1 which has *adhinvīt*. The currency of the *kṛṇva* form too up to this time is, perhaps, not to be questioned. But the Uṇādisūtras (149) derive kaṇva from kaṇ. This makes it appear possible that between the composition of the Dhātupāṭha and the Uṇādisūtras both pre-Pāṇinian *kṛṇva* had been an extremely rare form confined to the Paippalāda-Saṁhitā. Even here the position is anomalous, as both forms with -ṛ- and -a occur in the same sense in the Or MSS. But the restriction of the *kṛṇva* stem to a derogative sense is undeniable. We saw that there are ... instances of the employment of the term; all of them carry the derogative meaning. It is this special use, lost in later literature, which proves the one time existence of the term'

Pāṇini knew the AVP. Cf., the occurrence of the term *+pativatnī* (*patipatny-* Or., *pativinsy-* K in AVP 8.10.10 enjoined by Pāṇini in P.4.1.32. Patañjali enjoins this term under the same sūtra only for the Vedas.

That the term *kṛṇva* does not occur in the Aṣṭādhyāyī. This should have been caused by the absence of any occasion. Patañjali could have mentioned the form on 3.1.80. But he does not.

The word *kaṇva* twice occurs in the Aṣṭādhyāyī. P.3.1.17 is for the form kaṇvāyate 'does like kaṇva'. It seems to refer to the derogative meaning. 4.2.111 refers to the sage. But the vārtika to 3.1.14 mentions the word *kaṇvacikīrṣā*. It is is paraphrased in the Kāśikā as *pāpacikīrṣā* 'desire to do evil'. Kaiyaṭa adds in the Pradīpa on the same sutra *kaṇvaṁ pāpam ucyate* '*kaṇva* means evil'.

As to the position of Patañjali, even if he had known the form kṛṇva he could not do anything to a form, uncommon though, that he had received from the Vārtikakāra. Nor could he do anything to the received meaning of a word. He makes no comments.

Apart from that, the history of the Mahābhāṣya is largely obscure. It is said to have reduced to a single manuscript in the Deccan and gone out of use when Candrācārya rescued it from a mountainous country. This is supposed to have taken place in the 5th century AD. The historicity of this account has not been questioned. Possible mutations or loss occurring in the intervening period could have been responsible for the non-occurrence of the original word in the Mahābhāṣya which should have been *kṛṇvacikīrṣā*. Other explanations, too, are possible.

7

Works of Anundoram Borooah: An Appraisal

Ashok Kumar Goswami

yasyaiśvaryaṁ na cintyaṁ jagadidamakhilaṁ bhāsayatyuccamuccaṁ
yasyāstitvaṁ na dṛśyaṁ prakaṭitamaniśaṁ śobhanaṁ bhūtajātaiḥ/
vaicitryaṁ yasya sṛṣṭeh sphuṭamapiniyataṁ śakyate kena boddhuṁ
taṁ vande bhāvamūrtiṁ bhavamaraṇajaniṁ kāranaṁ kāraṇānām//

THIS IS THE *maṅgalācaranam* composed by Anundoram Borooah and occurring in the Volume III of his English Sanskrit Dictionary. With this, most respectfully I pay homage to the sacred memory of late Anundoram Borooah, one of the pioneer orientalists and a scholar extra ordinary of India in the nineteenth Century. Here is its translation:

> 'I pay homage to him, whose power is unthinkable, although it makes the entire creation exceedingly enlightened, whose existence is not visible, although it is ceaselessly superbly betrayed by the host of created beings, the wonders of whose creation although always explicit, cannot be understood by anybody, who has only an ideal existence, who is the cause of birth and death,

and who is the cause of all causes' (translation is from 'Anundoram Borooah' monograph by late Prof. Mukunda Madhava Sharma, page 96,—with gratitude).

The topic of today's lecture is 'The Works of Anundoram Borooah: An Appraisal'. Anundoram Borooah happens to be the first and foremost pioneer Indologist, eminent Sanskrit scholar of modern Assam. The deliberations on Anundoram Borooah's works, I trust, would provide an opportunity to the listenars to have the desired Tattvabodha to an extent. What is *Tattvabodha? Tasya bhāvah tattvaṁ, tattvasya bodhah tattvabodhah, tattvabodha* is the knowledge or understanding of the status, condition, nature or fact of *TAT* i.e. something or someone or some subject already known.

Apart from the general use of the word *tattvabodha* as already stated, there is the specific use of the word to stand for the knowledge of the essential nature of the Supreme entity. *Tattvabodha* or in another word *Tattvajnana* is used in spiritual contexts to give the sense of supreme knowledge. In the *Maṅgalacaraṇa* (Benedictory verse) of Anundoram Borooah I presented at the outset, Borooah gives a very high and ideal concept of God or the Supreme Entity. Let us now take a Quick Count of the Works of Anundoram in the chronological order.

1. Practical English Sanskrit Dictionary, published in three volumes
   Vol. I-1877
   Vol. II-1878
   Vol.III-1880
   Assam Publication Board (APB) published all the three volumes together in a Single Volume in 1971 under the title English Sanskrit Dictionary (ESD).
2. A Higher Sanskrit Grammar: Gender and Syntax (first as a supplementary treatise in the form of Preface to Esd II, later published independently in 1880).
3. On Ancient Geography of India: Geographical Names rendered in Sanskrit

(first as the preface to the ESD Vol. III, later on published independently by APB in 1971 under the title "Ancient Geography of India").

4. Mahaviracarita (MVC) (Barooah's own edition of Bhavabhui's first Rāma-play MVC along with self composed Sanskrit commentary *Jānakīrāmabhāṣya* (JRB) in 1877).
5. A Companion for Sanskrit Reading Undergraduates of Calcutta University, published in 1878, later published by APB under the title Selections from Sanskrit Classics.
6. Bhavabhuti and His Place in Sanskrit Literature, (planned for prefixing to MVC, actually published independently in 1878. APB published it first as preface to MVC in 1969, independently in 1971)
7. A Comprehensive Grammar of Sanskrit, Vol. X, 1887. Actually it was a work on prosody. So APB reprinted it, only as Prosody in 1969.
8. A single Volume Comprising editions of Vāmana's Kāvyālaṁkārasūtravṛtti, Vāgbhaṭa's Vāgbhaṭālaṁ-Kāra and Bhoja's Saraswatikaṇṭhābharaṇa (SKB) in 1883, later SKB separately published in 1884.
9. Hence SKB edition comes to be 9 in the list.
10. *Nānārthasaṁgraha* (NS): Published in 1884, NS is presented by Borooah as 'Vol. III of the Comprehensive Grammar of Sanskrit'. It is a traditional Dictionary.
11. *Dhātuvṛttisāra* (DVS): The full title as given by Borooah originally is *Dhātuvṛttisāra* or the Material Portion of the *Kātantragaṇavṛtti* with extracts from Ramānātha's Manoramā from Dhātukoṣa of Anundoram Borooah.
12. Amarasiṁha's *Nāmaliṅgānuśāsana* (NLS): This work is Borooah's English edition of Amara's *Nāmaliṅgānuśāsanam*, popularly known as *Amarakoṣa*, published first in 1887.

It is to be noted that Borooah's *Dhātukoṣa* (DK) or *Dhātupāṭha* is said to be completed in 1888, not known or found to be published.

A question is raised in the context of Borooah's incorporating HSG in ESD, Vol. II. How a book on Grammar can find place inside a Lexicon (a Dictionary)? Some scholars say that Borooah being aware of the link between Lexicon and Grammar found no difficulty in doing so. Actually Indian tradition draws no line of demarcation between Lexicon and Grammar, rather shows some sort of affinity between the two. In Amara's NLS, we find *Anuśāsana*, it is a work pertaining to 'Lexicon' class. Again in Patañjali's grammar book *Mahābhāṣyam*, we come across *Anuśāsana* in the introductory phrase—*atha śabdānuśāsanam* Similarly queries are possible in respect of inclusion of an essay on Geography i.e., *Ancient Indian Geography* inside ESD Vol. III and also in respect of Borooah's presenting his work on Sanskrit Prosody in the series of grammatical works projected as A Comprehensive Grammar of the Sanskrit Language. We shall take up the quarries in proper time.

Classification of Works

The classification of Borooah's works is possible as (1) Original Sanskrit Writings, (2) Critical Works on Classical Literature, (3) Textual Criticism, (4) Indological Studies, (5) Lexicographical Works, and (6) Grammatical Works.

Original Sanskrit Writing: *Jānakīrāmabhāṣya* (the Sanskrit Commentary to the drama *Mahāvīrācaritam* of Bhavabhūti), including eighteen verses in classical metres, Maṅgalācaraṇam (in English Sanskrit Dictionary, Vol. III, one verse), Mukhabandha (preamble), (in English Sanskrit Dictionary, Vol. II, five verses), Granthavisarjanam (dedication) (in English Sanskrit Dictionary, Vol. II, four verses), Dhātuvṛttisāra (two verses) (Total Sanskrit verses 30).

Critical Works on Classical Literature: This class covers *Bhavabhūti And His Place in Sanskrit Literature* (being a criticism on Rāma plays); Prosody (i.e. A Comprehensive Grammar of the Sanskrit Language Vol. X) (a Critical work on Sanskrit Prosody); the Composite Volume comprising Vāmana's *Kāvyālaṁkārasūtravṛtti*, Vāgbhaṭa's *Vāgbhaṭālṁkāra* and Bhoja's *Saraswatikaṇṭhabharaṇam* (being criticism on *Alaṁkāra* works).

Textual criticism: *Mahāvīracarita* (only work of this category).

Indological Studies: This category comprises the Ancient Geography of India and those portions of the Bhavabhūti And his Place in Sanskrit Literature, which deal with the identification of royal dynasties, ancient kingdoms and place—names.

Lexicographical Works: *Practical English Sanskrit Dictionary* (or English Sanskrit Dictionary), *Nānārthasaṁgraha*, Amarasiṁha's Nāmalīṇganuśasana, Dhātuvṛttisāra and Dhātukoṣa.

Grammatical Work: To a moderner *A Higher Sanskrit Grammar: Gender and Syntax* is the only grammatical work of Anundoram Borooah. But from the view point of tradition, his lexicographical works are also grammatical works. Tradition maintains that Lexicon is very much a part of Grammar. Here interestingly we can refer to Amara's entitlement of his *Amarakoṣa* as *Nāmaliṅgānuśāsana* (wherein there is *Anuśāsana*) and Patañjali's starting his grammatical Treatise *Mahābhāṣyam* with the statement *atha śabdānuśāsanam* (wherein also there is the word *anuśāsana*). Borooah's works obviously can be divided in the two groups—the Original and the Edited also.

Borooa's Thrust in Respect of Area or Category of Works:

Among various areas of pursuits, Borooah's Thrust was on Language-study that covers Lexical and Grammatical works.

How can we say so? He is found not to be a casual writer on grammar and Lexicon. He is found to follow the linguistic studies and research with a vision actuated by a higher philosophy vide his long observations in his Preface to *Prosody* (A Comprehensive Grammar of Sanskrit, Vol. X). The Main Points focused in the write up under reference are:

(i) It (the language) is the *Invaluable Inheritance* that has raised us (men) Unapproachably above other animals;
(ii) It is the inestimable BOON that props Our Social Organization and makes it Spiritualistic and God Reaching
(iii) Greater its influence, greater the Scale of Civilisation

(iv) Even in the most civilized countries, it is the Language that Directs men's Destiny and models our movements.

Thus Borooah arrests our attention to a very important Link between Spiritualization and Linguistic Culture.

I. *Works of Anundoram Borooah: Some details:*

Borooah's first work Practical English Sanskrit Dictionary as mentioned earlier was published in three volumes covering three parts. Part I—1877 (May), Part II—1878 (October) and Part III—1880 (June). Assam Publication Board (APB) published Borooah's three volumes of the Dictionary only as the *English Sanskrit dictionary* (ESD) covering 900 pages in 1971.

The Preface to the Volume II provided a supplementary treatise, A Higher Sanskrit Grammar: Gender and Syntax separately reprinted later on by APB. The Preface to the volume III of the Dictionary incorporated in it an essay on Geography entitled On Ancient Geography of India: Geographical Names rendered in Sanskrit. APB published the same separately in 1971 with a revised title, Ancient Geography of India.

While writing the Dictionary, after completing the first sixty four pages, Borooh sent the pages to the famous German Indologist Prof. Maxmullar for an opinion. Being encouraged by the hurriedly sent opinion of the Professor, Borooah was confidant to proceed and to persevere. In the preface to the first volume. Borooah disclosed the principles and the ideas to follow. Maxmullar opined that Borooah's Dictionary was going to be a safe and solid foundation for future works in the same direction.

It is proper to know at this stage that Monier William set the ball rolling in 1851 by bringing out his A Dictionary of English and Sanskrit. Borooah followed him in 1877, after a quarter of the century. Again Borooah was followed in 1884 by V.S. Apte who gave us Student's English Sanskrit Dictionary. Apte who derived much substantial assistance from Borooah's work, throws through his remarks sufficient light on relative merit of Borooah's Dictionary. In the preface to his own work, Apte observes: 'Borooah's work is eminently practical, it abounds with quotations from several standard authors, renderings generally happy. The work has a classical look; M. William's Dictionary is inferior to Borooah's in several respects. Apte frankly admits: 'My acknowledgements are chiefly due to Mr. Borooah'.

Dr. V. Raghavan, an eminent Sanskritist from Madras (presently Chennai) has observed in his foreword to Assam Publication Board's edition of Borooah's Dictionary (i. e. in English Sanskrit Dictionary) thus: Each of these three English Sanskrit Dictionaries of Moniar William, Anundoram Borooah and V.S. Apte, by Size, Range and Methodology, Borooah's work deserves *Commendation.*

The Hindu Patriot and the *English Man*, both of August 6, 1877 appreciated Borooah's Dictionary very highly.

In respect of quality of the work, Max Mullar's analysis deserves our attention: Addressing the author directly, he wrote:

Your work is evidently not simply a Sanskrit English Dictionary mechanically inverted; but you have treated each word independently and by giving the nearest approach to each English word in Sanskrit. You have shown your familiarity with idioms of both the languages. The passages from Sanskrit writers, illustrative of the employment of Sanskrit words are extremely useful and give your work a really scholar-like character (Academy, August 13, 1881).

A pertinent question is—What prompted Borooah to go for an English Sanskrit Dictionary instead of a Sanskrit English Dictionary? From Apte's remarks and News paper impressions, we come to understand that it was to encourage and enhance the Sanskrit writing among English knowing Indians. Though Borooah nowhere stated the purpose of composing the English Sanskrit Dictionary, he believed that Sanskrit words would be adequate for enriching the Indian Vernaculars. His composing Sanskrit verses and prose texts for the commentary were to show that Sanskrit had a potentiality to serve as medium of expressing nobler and higher ideas.

ESD: DISTINCTIVE FEATURES

For sake of giving Sanskrit equivalents, Borooah classified English words in three groups:

1. (i) Those for which there are or very near equivalents in Sanskrit e.g. causal = *hetumat*
   (ii) Those for which they are no equivalents, but the phrases in which they occur and the ideas which they convey are represented by different modes of expression on the basis of classical literature;
   (iii) Those which have evolved from new discoveries in Science and thought and for which words, there are no Sanskrit equivalents or equivocal modes of expression, e.g. Zoology = *Jivavijñānam.*
2. Another salient feature of Borooah's Dictionary is his Coining of New words. He did not hesitate to borrow from non-traditional and non-native sources. To illustrate—Soap = *Cāvaṇam,* gun = (i) cannon = *kāmānam* (ii) musket = *Bandukam,* gunman = kāmāntkah.
3. For rendering English words or idioms, Barooah wanted to provide Sanskrit Idioms.
   Nail Brush : Nakhamārjanī
   Tooth and nail = Ākeśāgrāt, Ānakhāgrāt

Borooah stated interestingly: "*Obsolete* and *technical* words of *rare* occurrence have no place in my dictionary".

In fine, it must be pointed out, Borooah took up writing an English Sanskrit Dictionary, presumably, to encourage English knowing or English reading Young Indians to go for Sanskrit writing. To inspire, he himself authored Sanskrit commentary comprising extensive Sanskrit prose and also verses in standard classical metres.

II. *A Higher Sanskrit Grammar: Gender and Syntax*

The work mainly deals with Gender and Syntax. Why? An impression was among the scholars, particularly among the westerners that Sanskrit Grammar was superior in many respects to any work of this kind produced anywhere in the world, professedly deficient in treatment of Syntax. This opinion was frankly expressed by H. Kern in his introduction to Sanskrit Syntax by J.S. Speijer. Borooah might have felt this deficiency and hence made this effort, or may be, he was very much interested in comparative philology. This attitude of Borooah is somewhat confirmed by his reference to Frenz Bopp, the founder of Comparative Philology in one of the five Sanskrit verses under the Heading *Mukhabandha* (Preamble) incorporated in the Grammar under discussion (Pat II of ESD):

> yāmāśritya bapā videśajaninodābhāvi śāstram navam/
> bhinnānām vacasām pradarśyasutarām sambandhasāram sphuṭam //

In this verse Borooah asserts that Bopp, the foreigner invented a new branch of learning by way of showing clearly the essential relationship among different speeches i.e. languages. Borooah's interest in comparative philology is seen in his giving in the Grammar book occasional equations with the rules of Greek and Latin.

Borooah resented that the work was to be prepared at mofussil, at places without library facility and no scope for consultation, hence possibility of there being mistakes.

However, the work of Borooah came to be highly accepted. As for instance, Speizer applauded Borooah's Grammar highly. Speizer also admitted his acknowledgements to Borooah in several respects in preparing his own work i.e. Sanskrit Syntax.

III. *Ancient Geography of India*

Borooah's preface of the Vol. IIIrd of *Practical English Sanskrit Dictionary*, in full title runs thus—'On Ancient Geography of India: Geographical names rendered in Sanskrit'. Assam Publication Board published this preface separately in 1984 under the title Ancient Geography of India, comprising 94 pages only.

Borooah's incorporation of this essay on Geographical data inside his dictionary comes to be accepted by Late Prof. M.M Sharma in his monograph *Anundoram Borooah* page 34 as he observes: As a part of the *English Sanskrit Dictionary* Borooah finds it necessary to give a "list of Geographical names with their Sanskrit representatives. This is done mostly by way of tracing back the ancient name for a modern place e.g. Bagmati>Bhogavati; Colapore>Karaviram,

Kolāpuram; Kanauj>Kānyakubjam so on. This requires a study of the Ancient Geography." This is why Borooah presents the results of his own research with the prefatory remark. "The subject has no doubt been ably handled by some foreign scholars of high celebrity. It ranks among its most successful and earnest devotees our great antiquarian General Alexander Cunningham. His work is *a standing monument of what a long useful life can achieve. But there are so many doubtful points that admitting my deep obligations to that accomplished scholar, I shall do best to give my own account of Ancient India."*

The observation of V.S. Apte, the lexicographer succeeding Borooah also testifies that Borooah's study on Geography is justified. "The third Appendix gives the most important names in the Ancient Geography of India ... and in this part of the work I have to cordially acknowledge the help I have derived from Cunningham's Ancient Geography, but particularly from Mr. Borooah's Essay."

Eminent historian Dr. S.K. Bhuyan, ex-Vice Chancellor of Gauhati University, observes in his biography of Anundoram Borooah in Assamese: Along with Sir Alexander Cunningham's monumental work on the subject, Anundoram's is regarded as the most valuable and I have seen editors and commentators of Sanskrit texts quoting Sri Borooah's authority in tracing the identity of places mentioned in our ancient classics.

In this book under discussion, Anundoram Borooah exhibits his profound knowledge of Mathematics, deep interest in Mathematics by way of explaining certain technical terms of the traditional treatise Līlāvati. It reminds us of Anundoram Borooah as a good student in Mathematics so as to secure highest marks in the subject in his I.A. Examination and 4th highest mark in the subject in the I.C.S. Examination. We notice Borooah's similar interest in Mathematics in the preface to his book *Prosody* (i.e. *A Comprehensive Grammar of Sanskrit,* Vol. X).

Prof. Max Muller, the great German Orientalist, in the *Academy* of 13 August, 1881 commented that Borooah's work on Ancient Geography of India would be gratefully received by the scholars of Europe. Cecil Bendal, had also remarked *Trubner's Record* in 1889 that the work is thoroughly original and a unique contribution to Indian research. In view of such comments Borooah came to observe in the concluding para of his work with a sense of gratification that 'his unpretentious labours are thoroughly appreciated by European fellow workers and my views have already received a French exponent in the Veteran scholar Mr. Felix Neve, Emeritus Professor in the University of LOUVAIN whose services to Sanskrit date from 1842.

IV. *Mahāvīracarita* (*MVC*)

- AB's MVC, published in 1877, is his text-critical edition of Bhavabhuti's drama *Mahāvīracarita*. The edition was with a self composed Sanskrit Commentary *Jānakīrāmabhāṣya* and also a Skt English *Glossary*.
- Borooah found that two available editions at his time were not adequate to satisfy the readers. It prompted him to go for an edition of his own. Those two already available editions were (i) one by Francis Henry Trithen in London, 1848 and the other by Taranath Tarkavacaspati in Calcutta, 1857. Borooah commented: none of these editions was accompanied by any *commentary*, or *translation* of the *Prākṛt* passages, absolutely necessary for the elucidation of the text, hence the move to remove the want, felt by all students (he added).
- Borooah added: No commentary of the *Vīracarita* was discovered till then. "So far as I am aware, there is no ancient commentary on this play' so Borooah's commentary came to be a very important one.

Comments:

(i) 'No hesitation in saying that your edition of *vīracarita* is the most valuable that we possess' – then principal of Calcutta Sanskrit College MM M.C. Nyāyaratna

(ii) It will be of much value to learners of Sanskrit – C.E. Bernard then Secretary to Govt. of India

(iii) Your *Viracarita* is the capital and of first water – Ramanath Saraswati, editor of *Rgveda*.

Jānakīrāmabhāsya (JRB)

This *Sanskrit* commentary by Borooah on Bhavabhuti's *MVC* is in the very *traditional* style. It is in *elegant prose* together with 18 *verses* in classical metres. As already stated finding no other commentary published till then, Borooah added himself this self composed commentary to his edition of MVC. The commemorative character of the commentary is clearly hinted in the following:

praṇamya jānakīrāmau sarabhāratapūjitau
jānakīrāmasaṁjñena bhāṣyena vivṛṇomyaham/
jānakīrāmasodaryo durlabhāgarganandanaḥ
ānandarāmabaduyā prāgjyotiṣpurasambhavaḥ//

Thereafter Borooah introduces his lamented brother Jānakīrām in four verses (to be quoted later here).

Following the practice of the traditional Sanskrit commentators of giving a name to their commentaries, Borooah also named his commentary (commentary hereafter) to MVC as the *Jānakīrāmabhāṣya*. The episode in the drama being related to Rāma and Sītā, the daughter of Janaka, the title is obviously appropriate. But by this title Borooah simultaneously made commemoration of his elder brother Jānakīrām Borooah who passed away earlier.

Cf. *śrīmadānandarāmeṇa durlabhāgargasūnunā/*
atikrāntena kaumāram kaumāro vivṛto mudā//

Bhavabhūti gave a name to each of the cantos of the drama like Kaumāra etc. Keeping conformity with Bhavabhūti's naming of each act, Anundoram Borooah gave a verse at the end of his commentary to each act. As for illustration in the verse quoted, the word Kaumāra, 2nd word in 2nd line is a name given by Bhavabhūti to the act concerned.

JRB is undoubtedly a work of exquisite diction and captivating music. To illustrate the point, here I quote some commemorative verses:

āsīnme dayito bhrātā jānakīrāmaviśrutaḥ /
pitroḥ priyataraḥ putraḥ prāgjyotispuranandanaḥ //
aṁkeśabde purāvṛtte labdhavistīrṇavodhanaḥ /
svadeśasya hite kārye sadā pravanamānasaḥ //

The commentary is full of allusions, parallel quotations and critical elucidations of grammatical points. At the same time, it is very easy and it does not lack in references to modern situations whenever necessary.

V. *Selections from Sanskrit Classics*

The work was originally published in 1877 by Anundoram Borooah under the title *A companion for the Sanskrit reading Undergraduates of the Calcutta University* (CU). APB reprinted the book with the new title, Selections from Sanskrit Classics (SSC). The Sanskrit syllabus (CU) for F.A. and B.A. prescribed Meghadutam, Abhijñānaśakuntalam, Kirātārjunīyam (Cantos 1–5). Kumārasambhavam (Cando 1–7) and Raghuvaṁśam (Cantos 1–9), Borooah had some reservations on C.U. Sanskrit syllabus, particularly he was not happy with C.U.'s prescribing Bhaṭṭikāvyam which he thought to be tough for the young students. Borooah considered it as an undue pressure on young learners. Borooah in his work provided notes, criticism and other observations on important aspects of the prescribed texts.

By his work Borooah wanted to arouse a curiosity in the minds of the students so that they could exert themselves to extract the proper meanings of the Sanskrit verses and sentences of their own instead of blindly accepting the arguments and views of the ancient scholars.

Why is this expectation? What is in his mind?

Borooah was of the view that in the context of advancement of modern civilization and knowledge, the Sanskrit verses etc. should be interpreted in the new light. He also opined that by such careful endeavour that we can eliminate the utter apathy of the present-day Indians towards the ancient literature of India.

Some observations

Borooah's attitude towards traditional scholars should not be mistaken in view of his aforesaid expectation. Yes, Borooah was not prepared to depend solely upon them. Anundoram Borooah frankly stated, "I by no means think lightly of some of these commentators. I have the greatest respect for Mallinatha. He is certainly the best, most learned and most faithful of Sanskrit text expositors." In writings of Borooah, no any adverse comment against traditional scholars has come to our notice, but he felt that (a) in the matter of scientific investigation, a modern scholar has the advantage over a traditional commentator; (b) this expectation as well as his criticism in the book under discussion bring to light Borooah's habit of self criticism and love of reason. (c) the work SSC came to be well accepted in the scholarly as well as in readers' circles, (d) has shown the modern method of studying Sanskrit, (e) remarks of Cecil Bendal, the keeper of oriental books in the British Museum, 'most useful for European students' because of Borooah's middle course treatment, (f) no lapse noticed in respect of propriety, arguments are very sound, (the book) reveals author's originality, very well written by the man of great learning (comments by)—SAMPRAKASH.

Anundoram Borooah's Opposition to Learn by Rot

"There can be no doubt that the little progress made in the tols of our country is owing to the method of study pursued—to the prominence given to getting by heart grammatical aphorism and lexicographical verse and to extreme neglect of the more important sphere of intellect. I have every confidence that much better results would be achieved if Sanskrit Grammar is more philosophically and systematically studied and proper care is taken in thoroughly impressing on the students—the true sense and full force of the texts they read"—preface to SSC.

The above quoted observation of Borooah in the context deserves our attention.

VI. *Bhavabhūti and His Place in Sanskrit Literature* (*BHPSL*)

(1) Anundoram Borooah published BHPSL in the beginning of 1878. APB reprinted it first in 1969 as an *introduction to MVC, independently* in 1971.

(2) Anundoram Borooah's BHPSL is the pioneering work in *Modern Criticism of Dramas* in Sanskrit.

(3) The text contains—*comparative study* of the *three plays* of Bhavabhūti MVC URC MM in respect of Common Verses, expressions, passages, Language and Thought.

(4) Anundoram Borooah opines that Bhavabhūti was first to dramatize Rāma (to write drama on Rāma theme). Borooah could say so as till Borooah's time, many other plays, particularly *the plays ascribed* to Bhāsa *were yet to be discovered.*

(5) BHPSL, as occasions demanded, is found to cover

  (a) The chronology of the Rāma plays and that also of *Naiṣadhacarita, Kāvyaprakāśa, Sāhityadarpaṇa Daśarūpaka,* SKB (of Bhoja) etc.,

  (b) Comparative assessment of *Raghuvaṁśa* and *Bhaṭṭikāvya.*

(6) Specifically determines the date and place of Bhavabhūti, *Comparative* study of *Kālidāsa* and *Bhavabhūti,* their relative *chronology, relative* chronology of three plays (MVc, URC and MM).

(7) General survey of Rāma plays (Hanuman nāṭaka, *Rāmāyaṇa & Bhattikavya, Kundamālā, Jānakīharaṇa, Rāghavābhyudaya, Rāghavavilāsa, Udāttarāghava, Anargharāghava, Prasanna-rāghava,* URC, MVC).

(8) Examines in MVC condition of Women, geography of the time

(9) Vocabulary & defects of the dramas

(10) A critical appreciation of URC BHPSL (2)

(11) Opinion that Mālatimādhava (MM) is the best of Bhavabhūti's dramas,

(12) Bhavabhūti's genus highlighted—Western appreciation:

Yes, Bhavabhūti's prophesy came true. Being disappointed by the cool attitude from his contemporaries, Bhavabhūti resented with a prophesy.

ye nāma kecidiha naḥ prathayantyavajñām
jānanti te kimapi tān prati naiṣa yatnaḥ/

utpatsyate 'sti ko 'pi samānadharmā
kālo 'hyayaṁ niravadhirvipulā ca pṛthvī||

(Can those who regard me with disdain claim to know me? I have not labored for their sake. There will be in future or is at present someone somewhere who is equal to me, because time is indeed endless and the world is vast).

Western scholars are of the opinion that Anundoram Borooah could assess Bhavabhūti in actuality. He maintained that Bhavabhūti had an appeal to him more than anybody else. In view of AB's extraordinary appreciation of Bhavabhūti, Bhavabhūti's prophecy came *true*.

Borooah in the Context of Date of Bhavabhūti

Ghanashyam, the traditional commentator of *Uttararāmacaritam*, accepted Bhavabhūti as the contemporary of Kālidāsa and a court poet of Bhojarāja. Kalhana, the author of Rājatarangiṇī accepted the dramatist as the court poet of king Yaśovarma of Kanauj (8th century A.D.). In the opinion of P.V. Kane, the literary activity of Bhavabhūti may be assigned to first quarter of the 8th century A.D. We may take few years more, to place him in the 2nd part of that century. Dr. R.G. Bhandarkar is also of the same view.

Anundoram Borooah, on the other hand fixes the date of Bhavabhūti in the 5th century A.D. Anundoram Borooah is the first scholar to apply a modern method in determininig a date. His deliberations in this context cover comparative chronology of Kālidāsa and Amarasiṁha. He maintains that Bhavabhūti was a successor to Kālidāsa, but he must be predecessor to Amarasimha as Borooah used words like *Kaṁkāla*, which are irregular and unacceptable to Amara. Again as there was decline of Buddhism from the 5th century onwards and the female Buddhist ascetics appeared on the stage in the drama '*Mālatīmādhavam*' without meeting with any rebuke Borroah wants to conclude that Bhavabhūti flourished not later than the 5th century A.D. Another argument of Borooah is that Bhavabhūti openly refers to some ancient Hindu rites 'shocking to modern Hindu ideas'. In his two Rāma plays viz. MVC & URC which also confirms his views asserting the 5th century as the date of Bhavabhūti.

VII. *Prosody*

This is the Assam Publication Board edition of Borooah's *A Comprehensive Grammar of the Sanskrit Language* Vol. X. As Anundoram's present work covered only prosody, Assam publication Board brought out its edition entitled as '*Prosody*' only.

In the prospectus issued earlier in respect of the project on a comprehensive Grammar, he already stated that the volume on *Prosody* would come first. He maintained that. Though brought out first in the series, he named it X Vol, for reasons not known to us.

Now we find a work on Prosody included in a series on Grammar. Here as we remember, tradition in respect of six Vedāṅgas keeps *chandaḥ* (prosody) and *Vyākaraṇa* (grammar) as different cf. *chandaḥ pādau tu vedānām mukhaṁ vyākaraṇam smṛtam*. Incorporating a work on prosody in a grammar series, Anundoram Borooah maintains that prosody is the most important branch of Sanskrit Grammar. He sees the greatest utility of prosody in removing, to quote in his words, "All faults of omission, insertion and alteration; for reconstructing traditional texts" Prof. M.M. Sharma understands that it is in the interest of Textual ciricism (Vide Sharma's book *Anundoram Borooah*, MMS, p.42).

Contents of the Work Prosody

(a) Preface: History of Sanskrit Prosody,

(b) (i) Sanskrit text of the *Chandaḥsūtra* of Piṅgala, translation and critical expansion of the *Sūtras* in eight chapters.

 (ii) Casually quotation from the Ṛkprātiśākhya of Śaunaka;

 (iii) We come across example of lengthy explanation, say four pages for Piṅgala.

(c) Now comes Borooah's main dissertation called PROSODY, an independent treatise on the science of Sanskrit Prosody in five parts, viz. Preliminary, Vedic metres, classical syllabic metres (*akṣarachandaḥ*), quantitative metres (*mātrāchandaḥ*) and

Pause (*Yati*), All the known Vedic and classical metres are defined and explained in English.

It is to be noted that prosody is 'designed as a text book'.

VIII. *Vāmana's Kāvyālaṁkārasūtravṛtti & Vāgbhaṭa's Vāgbhaṭālaṁkāra*

The next work of Barooah in chronological order is Vāmana's *Kāvyālaṁkārasūtravṛtti*, *Vāgbhaṭālaṁkāra* and Bhoja's *Saraswatikaṇthā-bharaṇa*, published in a composite volume in 1883. The third poetic work in the volume i.e. Bhoja's *Saraśwatīkaṇṭhābharaṇa* was later separately published by reducing the price to make easily purchasable by poor teachers and students of Sanskrit.

The first work of the composite volume is Vamana's *Kāvyālaṁkarasūtravrtti* which covers 48 pages for the main text, preceded by an *Anukrama* (table of contents), Notes, corrections, Reading (e.g. variant readings). The notes are in Sanskrit, being simple elucidations given by Borooah himself.

The second book in the volume is Vāgbhaṭa's *Vāgbhaṭālaṁkāra*. The main text covers 24 pages, preceded by extracts from Siṁhadeva Gani's Commentary, *Anukrama* (table of contents), Reading i.e. variant readings and corrections.

As stated already, the third work in the composite volume i.e. Bhoja's *Saraswati kaṇṭhābharaṇa* (SKB) came to be published separately. The separately published SKB of Bhoja came to be Book No. 9 of Borooah in chronological order.

IX. *The Volume Comprising Edition Only of* Sarasvatīkaṇṭhābharaṇa

Being separated from the other two poetic works namely KLSV and *Vāgbhatalaṁkāra* (Vol. 8). The purpose of separate publication is made clear in the preface (January 18, 1884).

"It has been represented to me that many of the students of Sanskrit such as those of Bhatpara, and Mulajor cannot avail themselves of my edition of SKB on account of its high price. I accordingly reissue it at a greatly reduced price."

(i) He regretted failure to bring out the full text with a full commentary because of being busy. Here we gather the impression that Borooah always had sympathy for poor Sanskrit students. Borooah's anxiety to improve upon the texts in hinted also by this statement. "Should I succeed hereafter in procuring mss of all the text I want, I shall try to remove these defects, if suitable opportunity occurs."

SKB is a voluminous work on poetics composed by Bhojarāja. The APB edition of SKB alone covers 352 pages—text followed by 24 pages of notes, which mainly provide (a) grammatical notes on difficult words, Sanskrit renderings of all the *Prakrit* passages (Prose) and verses (b) sources of all the quotations given in illustrations, The Notes given in Tika form in Sanskrit appear to be the product of Erudition and Hard Labour. According to Anundoram Borooah, Bhoja's SKB is the best of the works on poetics. But its terse language and subtle classifications come to hinder its popularity.

X. *Nānārthasaṁgraha*

Borooah's Nānārthasaṁgraha (NS) is his A Comprehensive Grammar of Sanskrit, Vol. III. The book was originally published in 1884, later reprinted by APB in 1969. It is a traditional Lexicon in Sanskrit. Notwithstanding there being several works of this kind already, Borooah moved for this work in order to eliminate anomalies noticed by him in the existing works. NS was issued by Borooah as the first part of the 3rd volume of his projected 12 Vol. Comprehensive Grammar.

NS is a Dictionary of Homonyms presented in an alphabetic order along with meanings. The meanings are presented in the form of judicious and select quotations from as many as twelve classical Lexicons. Borooah took pains to examine the relevant Modern Dictionaries, works of Traditional Lexicon, various commentaries on them in order to authenticate the meanings. The compilation covers 5,500 key words. Homonyms are accompanied by *Śabdabhedaprakāśikā*, a chapter from Maheśvara's *Viśvaprakāśa*.

Contents of the chapter under reference in brief:

(1) Words having the same meaning with slight difference in spelling, e.g., vikāśa and vikāsa, jumbuka and jambūka.

(2) Words which should have 'Va' and not 'b' (i.e. labiodental and not labial)

(3) Words which should have 'b' and not 'va' (labial and not labiodentals) e.g. *brndāraka*

(4) Words having difference in being cerebral, dental and palatal.

A section specifying the genders of words.

XI. *Dhātuvṛttisāra*

Dhātuvṛttisāra (DVS) was originally published in 1877 and later reprinted by APB in 1977. The full title of the work is *Dhātuvrttisāra* or Material Portion of Kātantra Gaṇavṛtti with extracts from Ramānātha's Manoramā from the *Dhātukosa* of Anundoram Borooah (as originally given by Borooah).

The DVS is actually a part of Anundoram Borooah's *Dhātukoṣa* (DK) written by the author depending on the *Kātantragaṇavṛtti*, a Grammar by Durgāsiṁha, in which all Sanskrit roots are classified in ten classes (*Daśagaṇa*), and each root is named with its meaning. No *Dhātukoṣa* by some other author gives such a systematic presentation of verbal roots.

Illustration of the presentation

> *'bhū sattāyām sato bhāvaḥ pravṛtinimittam sattā; bhavati kedāresvaṅkuraḥ.*

English rendering: The root bhū is used in the sense of existence (*sattā*), *sattā* is the state of being existent or the very reason of being existent. The verb *bhavati* derived from the root *bhū* is illustrated with the sentence *'bhavati kedāresu aṅkuraḥ'* (sprout of grass exists in the field).

DVS is completely in Sanskrit, not a single English word is given a place in the work.

The work was authored by Borooah only for teachers and students of the Tols, price for common readers was Rs. 2/-, half for poor students.

A Sanskrit colophon in two verses occurs at the end in which Borooah begs apology for possible mistakes or lapses which might occur due to inaccuracies in the MSS and ignorance of the compositors, c.f. *bahūni skhalitānyatra pustakānāmaśuddhitaḥ/ yojakānām ca bāliśyam prasādaye //*

XII. *Nāmaliṅgānuśāsana*

Anundoram Borooah's *Nāmaliṅgānuśāsana* is his edition of Amarasiṁha's *Nāmaliṅgānuśāsanam,* popularly known as the *Amarakoṣa.* The work was originally published in 1887, reprinted by APB in 1987.

Amara's *Nāmaliṅgānuśāsanam* (NLS) is the oldest lexicographical work in Sanskrit and for centuries has condinued to be infallible guide for all learners of Sanskrit.

As we know Borooah committed the whole Koṣa to memory early in childhood at the instance of his father and hence it is not unusual to find him with an urge to bring out an edition of his own. But it is not a stereotyped edition, rather a Text Critical Edition that is also in English. The reason is not far to seek. Borooah himself discloses: such an English critical edition was considered Desideratum both in India and Europe, by scholars like Eggling.

NLS consists of three Kāṇḍas i.e. three books dealing with Synonyms, together with three appendices dealing with Homonyms, Indeclinable and Gender. Borooah planned to bring out the work in three parts, published the first part in 1887, second in the next year; but he could not bring out the third part as death snatched him away. But even this partial publication brought to him great appreciation from the eminent Sanskritists as well as from leading Newspapers of the time.

All found special value in the preface to the Edition. All admired his immense industry, untold labour in collecting Amara's MSS with important commentaries from different places like India Office Library (London), Deccan College (Poona), Benaras, Cittagonj, Durgapur and other places.

Prior to Borooah, none could collect the commentary of Khirasvami. This commentary on Amara is the oldest and most important one. Scholars were all praise for Borooah.

After all, Borooah's NLS is a very fine specimen of text critical edition of Ancient Texts.

XIII. *Dhātukoṣa* (*DK*) (*some observations*)

- AB's last work comes as entitled Dhātukoṣa or Dhātupātha recorded as published in 1888.
- But the book could not be available to us.
- APB has not published or reprinted;
- DR SK Bhuyan gave long account of all books of AB excepting DK, reference *only by name*
- Late Prof. M.M. Sharma's admission—'all his searches for a copy of the book in possible sources of Poona (Pune) and Calcutta (Kolkata) went in vain'.
- Yes, AB had referred to the book (i) described his DVS as 'from the Dhātukosa of AB'. (ii) twice he referred to DK in his NLS (Amara)

Probability

- Could not have complete publication, at his last days, still in a printing stage
- Confirmation of our Surmise

Cecil Bandal, the keeper of Oriental books at British Museum, in his obituary note (after Borooah's demise).

"What is this *Dhātupātha*? A projected work of Anundoram?...... I should be obliged if any friend of the deceased scholar would inform me on this point, in order that the book may be properly 'catalogued' in the 'supplementary Sanskrit catalogue which I am preparing for the British Museum'.

XIV. *Anundoram Borooah and Sanskrit*

Borooah was a bar-at-law and a highly placed I.C.S. Officer. What then prompted Borooah to choose Sanskrit as the medium of intellectual culture? What made him interested in Sanskrit studies and research? Obviously our answer will be that he came to be attracted by the Magic of the language. The magic of Sanskrit lies in the Potency of the language and in the beauty of the literature. In the words of Anundoram, he was 'overwhelmed by the grand Museum of the Sanskrit Philology'. We can take note of Borooah's impressions of and attitude towards Sanskrit here:

(1) He views Sanskrit as "the most copious, most refined, most philosophical language" (vide "*Selections From Sanskrit Classics*").

(2) He observed: "To me Sanskrit is dearer than any other language".

(3) "Its music has charms which no words can express".
Its capability of representing every form of human thought in most appropriate language is probably not rivaled, certainly not surpassed by any other language".

(4) "Most touching scenes have been drawn in heartrending words, most noble images have been clothed in most sublime languages, most terrific pictures have been couched in terror-producing expressions" (observed thus in the concluding part of the work – *Bhavabhūti and His place in Sanskrit Literature*).

(5) His another observation in the preface to the work, *Prosody* is noteworthy for us: "I shall consider my time most usefully employed if my work can evoke in India an earnest regard for our ancient literature and a sincere desire to strive honestly to seek out noble truth."

In fine, I appeal to our young scholars to take interest in the great and valued contributions of Anundoram Borooah, which deserve and demand serious attention from us.

I now seek to the close with the presentation of Anundoram Borooah's Eulogy of mother language Sanskrit, occurring in the *mukhabandha* (preamble) in the Vol. II of his ESD.:

yasyāmādikaviḥ pavitracaritaṁ rāmasya divyaṁ byadhāt
yasyāścitrarasā vicitraracanā bābhāti kādambarī /
yā bhāsye gahanām dhiyaṁ vitanute 'bhīśam parāṁ śāṅkare
jīvyāt sāpralayaṁ samujjvalatarā saṁskārapūtāgirā//
yasyai suddhavibuddhasaugatamataṁ prthvyā mahaddhāryate
reme taimuravamśabhusanamatīvānandayitryā yayā/
yā śarmanyakavīśacittamaharad granthena tena ksanāt
sā no bhāratabhāratī śrutisudhāṁ sarvatra kīryāt sadā//

8

Persian Painting: A Reminiscence of the Cultural Past

S. P. Verma

I. *Persian Painting*

> Persian painting is mainly an art of decorative book-illustration, and in it, as in most excellence-miniature painting, narrative power is a necessary part of book.
>
> J.V.S. Wilkinson (1930)

THE OLDEST EXAMPLES of Persian painting (mainly hunting and battle scenes) are the wall-paintings at Keh-i-khwaja (Sistan) of first century A.D. Next in order of chronology are the paintings on walls of palaces of Sassasian period, 226–642 A.D.

The introduction of Islam as religion of Persia restricted the scope of painting and the earliest miniature like painting are found on pottery of about 1200 A.D.

The earliest manuscript with illustrations date from the late thirteenth to the middle of fourteenth century, during the Mongol period. Most of these manuscripts are historical accounts, *Shahnama* manuscript. This first phase of Persian painting is identified with Mongol style.

New style emerged in the second half of fourteenth century and lasted through fifteenth century – usually called 'Timurid style', flourished under the great patrons: Shah Rukh (1377–1447) Baysunghur Mirza (1397–1434), and Iskandar (1384–1414). During this period aside the great work, *Shahnama*, the books of great poets Nizami, Sa'di and others were mostly illustrated.

The main ateliers were: Shiraz, Herat and Tabriz. Culmination of this style is found in the work of Bihzad (active, 1480–1536) who was active mainly at the court of Herat, under the last Timurids. The style of Bihzad and his school lingered on in Bukhara until the middle of 16th century.

Under the Safavaid Shahs, the Timunid style continued, but under Shah Tahmasp I (1514–1576) realistic scenes and album pictures became frequent. Later during 17th century, during the reign of Shah Abbas I (1557–1629) there emerged revival of wall paintings in royal and public buildings. Muhammadi, Aqa Riza, Riza'-i Abbasi and Mu'in are great artists of Safavid school. The centres of Safavid paintings were Qazwini, Tabriz, Shiraz. Herat, Meshhed and Isfahan.

Towards the end of the 17th century there began to appear direct imitations of European subjects and techniques as a result of Muhammad Zaman's visit to Italy (during the reign of Shah Abbas II, 1642–1666) and during the 18th century illustration in manuscripts but was almost entirely abandoned were large paintings, mostly portraits in oils in vogue.

A revival took place during the reign of Fath Ali Shah (1798–1834) and some fine miniatures were produced at his court but it never attained the Timurid level of art. The manuscripts of *Shahnama* and *Khamsa* of Nizami were most frequently illustrated. However, under the patronage of Qazr dynasty whose capital was Teheran, a new style of oil painting, owing greatly to European art was started. Gradually full-fledged acceptance of European manner of painting dislodged the Persian painting.

II. *Painting, a pictorial document of Cultural Past*

Art is a mirror of society. In other words, it is a visual commentary on man's life and his activities, and it is possible to reconstruct the history of the material culture of the people in rich and vivid form from sculptures and paintings. In view of the vast store of information on our past that comes from the written sources, we tend to forget that pictorial depictions proceed pictographs and ideographs, the early forms of writing. In pictorial depictions on stone in caves and rock shelters man has left unique records of how he hunted and gathered food.

Of late there has been emphasis on the social and cultural history of the people, their daily life and work. In paintings we have more intimate view of material life than we can see anywhere else. In the chronicles, the story of the life of people remains largely untold.

In view of the problems that are characteristic of research in history, especially those relating to the source-material, the need of finding out new sources for discovering facts cannot be overemphasized. Whereas the greater mass of textual and archaeological source-material available enables us to reconstruct a plausible picture of political and social life, the problem of cultural history is by and large still incomplete. This could be met by extracting evidence from sculptures, paintings, epigraphs, archaeological remains, artifacts and the like.

Pictorial representations, especially those with the graphic description of details of an object deserve utmost attention of the historians. They acquire greater importance from the fact that they contain visual information of events and things that we may not ordinarily get in chronicles. In many instances, visual narratives are very detailed and frank. Even the commonest articles representing material culture are met with, testifying to the intimate observation of the painters. In the absence of the textual evidence, nothing can be of greater value than contemporary pictorial records: sculpture and painting. Through this medium we find, in illustrated form, a variety of evidence that supplements or explains textual descriptions. The importance is still greater, when there is paucity of information in textual source-material. The pictorial evidence comes to us in the form of sculptures, frescoes, and miniatures, both in albums and manuscripts. These illustrate people's daily life, artisans and professionals at work with their tools and implements. Fortunately, the medieval period is the richest in this respect. The Persian rulers/ patrons maintained calligraphers, painters and book binders, etc. consequently, we have fairly continuous record of their works. A good many of these have been lost; yet those surviving provide us ample material for studying the culture of the times.

Numerous Persian miniatures exhibit outdoor scenes that present various aspects of people's life. The subject treated include masons and labourers at work, gardeners tending to orchards, peasant ploughing the field, woman working on spinning wheel, cooking and milking the cow or a sheep, musicians and dancers giving their performances, cooks, sufis, and *faqirs*, etc. These miniatures are indispensable source of information about the life in past. As a matter of fact looking at these pictures is like living in those times itself.

Quite importantly, pictorial representations often help us in correcting the perspective gathered from literary sources only. We know that the history of technology can never be adequately written without the aid of visual projections through paintings and drawings. The absence of actual specimens enhances the importance of pictorial representations. The survival of wooden material, at least, is very unlikely. In the absence of actual remains of the object, pictorial representations must always occupy a very important place. The importance is still greater when textual evidence is limited and pictorial representations constitute our sole evidence in the form of sculptures, frescoes, and miniatures.

Scenes depicting battles, sieges, feast, festivities, and the like provide evidence on the performance of the imperial *naqqarkhana*. These bear testimony to the types and forms of a variety of musical instruments which formed an integral part of the royal drum-house, such as *naqqara, surna qarna, saj*, and *nafir*. The *daf, chang rubab, alghoza*, harp, and castanets are other musical instruments shown in the accompaniment to female dancers.

Miniatures illustrating battles and sieges further depict a variety of arms and armour. The armour of war animals, horses, and elephants, are also vividly portrayed. Apart from the conventional arms heavy and light pieces of artillery and the matchlocks depicted in the miniatures refer to their earlier shape and mechanism. Such evidence of the past becomes practically decisive for the history of firearms. The ensigns of royalty, in vogue during medieval times and represented in the paintings, too, are of our interest.

Further, the miniatures illustrating feast and festivities containing the depiction of utensils used for cooking and serving the preparations, cutlery, and a variety of bottles (*surahi*, etc.), perfume–pots, and candle-sticks, etc. are the major sources for study.

Paintings provide a fine source of information related to the sartorial habits of the people of all classes from the aristocracy to the peasant. To sum up, illustrations of the historical events, and authentic portraits of rulers, poets, artists, and scribes, etc. are the reminiscence of the past.

There are many more items which can be studied in greater detail with the help of illustrated manuscripts. In fact, the illustrations of the well known epic *Shahnama*, legend *Kalilah wa Dimnah*, poems of Nizami, Sa'di and others, and the historical accounts are extensive store of information relating to the material culture. The present attempt is only a humble step to understand the significance of Persian painting as a viable source for the people's history.

9

Accessing Manuscripts in the Digital Age
Hypertext Presentation, Cataloguing, and Text-Image Alignment

Peter M. Scharf

Abstract. Access to Sanskrit manuscripts is severely hampered by distance to collections, isolation of artifacts from complementary research materials, deficiency or lack of metadata, and disarray within collections and within individual items of a collection. Arranging, cataloguing, scanning, and web-hosting of digital images of artifacts obviously address these problems. Yet an additional impediment confronts users of web-based primary literary sources in Indian languages: information processing technology that has developed primarily in the environment of the Roman alphabet is incompatible with non-European languages. Non-alphabetic scripts, multiple scripts, unusual orthographic conventions that hide word boundaries, and highly inflected and agglutinative language structures resist conventional digital technologies that take uniform European linguistic representations for granted. As a result, the normal functionality of finding aids is inadequate to cope with Indian collections. An additional problem in dealing with hand-written materials as opposed to digital or printed materials is the greater time and effort required to navigate the text in the manuscript. Manuscripts must be used on site in special collection rooms usually isolated from related materials. Hence, sought passages are difficult and time-consuming to find. The Sanskrit Library has developed protocols, formats, and software to overcome linguistic impediments and to provide web access to the primary cultural heritage materials of India. Materials developed include a comprehensive integrated hypertext catalogue and software to integrate digital images of manuscript pages with the corresponding machine-readable text thereby providing direct and focused access to specifically sought passages on individual manuscript pages. The facilities for searching expected of contemporary web interfaces is thus extended to digital manuscript images and the path opened for generalized information extraction and search techniques to reach Sanskrit manuscripts.

Keywords: India, Sanskrit, manuscripts, digital images, catalogue, text-image alignment, computational linguistics

1. *Crisis in the transmission of inherited knowledge*

The enormous heritage of knowledge and culture in the form of manuscripts written in Sanskrit in India is under threat of extinction as the dominant medium for the transmission of knowledge shifts and the lifespan of extant manuscripts approaches expiration. Already the shift from handwriting to print drew practices and resources away from the culture of manuscripts. The current shift from the printed medium to the digital medium further marginalizes manuscripts as the expected methods of accessing information depart further from the norms of the manuscript culture. The National Mission for Manuscripts and forward-looking manuscript libraries around the world have recognized the importance of surveying, cataloguing, and making digital images of extant manuscripts as well as of encouraging critical text-editing. Yet the digital medium offers many facilities that could be engaged to enhance access to these valuable artifacts of Indian heritage if technologies are adapted and extended to cope with the features of these items. A glance at the history of the preservation and loss of knowledge in prior media transitions and the adaptation of technologies necessitated in order to preserve knowledge during such transitions offers some insight into what is required to preserve the knowledge in manuscripts in the current transition to the digital medium. An investigation of such issues prompted the Sanskrit library to undertake to adapt standards and develop formats, protocols and innovative technologies to enhance access to manuscripts in the digital age. We adapted the Unicode standard, articulated phonetic encodings of Sanskrit, created transcoding software to and from various input and display methods, wrote linguistic software, and created a pipeline for dynamic cataloguing and text-image alignment in order to provide integrated digital access to Sanskrit manuscripts. The Sanskrit Library is eager to share its expertise in this area to help to preserve the inherited knowledge and culture of India and to propagate it for future generations.

1.1 Sanskrit literature

Sanskrit is the primary culture-bearing language of India, with a continuous production of literature in all fields of human endeavor over the course of four millennia. Preceded by a strong oral tradition of knowledge transmission, records of written Sanskrit remain in the form of inscriptions dating back to the first century B.C.E. In surveys to date, the National Mission for Manuscripts has already counted more than five million manuscripts, and David Pingree, the renowned manuscriptologist and historian of mathematics, estimated that extant manuscripts in Sanskrit number over 30 million—more than one hundred times those in Greek and Latin combined—constituting the largest cultural heritage that any civilization has produced prior to the invention of the printing press. Sanskrit works include extensive epics, subtle and intricate philosophical, mathematical, and scientific treatises, and imaginative and rich literary, poetic, and dramatic texts. While the Sanskrit language is of preeminent importance to the intellectual and cultural heritage of India, the importance of the intellectual and cultural heritage of India to the rest of the world during the past few millennia and in the present era can hardly be overestimated. It has been a major factor in the development of the world's religions, languages, literature, arts, sciences, and history. The tradition of Vedic recitation, dating to the second millennium B.C.E., was declared by the United Nations Educational, Scientific and Cultural Organization (UNESCO) in November 2003 to be one of the "masterpieces of the oral and intangible heritage of humanity" under a program aiming to raise public awareness of the value of this heritage and encourage governments to take legal and administrative steps to safeguard it. In the first millennium B.C.E. trade flourished between India and the Achaemenid Empire, Hellenistic empires, and the Roman Empire. In the early centuries C.E., political, educational, and religious leaders brought Indian literature and culture to Southeast Asia. Buddhist missionaries brought Indian culture to Tibet, Central Asia, and China, and from there to Korea and Japan. Through the intermediary of Muslim scholarship, and Latin and Greek translations of it in the eleventh, twelfth, and thirteenth centuries, Indian astronomy, astrology, mathematics, medicine, philosophy, and literature served as the sources of the revival of civilization in the Latin West and in Byzantium. Indian ideas permeate the scientific texts of the high Middle Ages from which modern Western science and literature directly descend.

1.2 The crisis

Manuscripts in India are kept in a variety of conditions ranging from climate controlled libraries in university campuses, government institutions, or esteemed societies, to temple libraries, private libraries, and small caches in private homes. In many of the latter types of repositories they are exposed to a range of temperatures, high humidity and are unprotected from insects and worms. The physical support of manuscripts in India is generally palm leaf in the South and paper in the North. These materials last for 300–500 years. More than half the lifespan of most manuscripts has already expired. The tradition of copying manuscripts by hand diminished steadily after the introduction of moveable type in India in the last quarter of the 18th century and has now all but ceased.

The number of both traditional and modern scholars of Sanskrit is diminishing both within and outside India with the lapse of time and changing educational trends. In India the status of Sanskrit in most school systems has receded to that of a foreign language. Abroad primary and secondary education remains grossly undersupplied with adequate educational materials about India so that few students are aware of its rich and abundant literature. Manuscript materials are completely inaccessible to students at these lower levels. As a result of low awareness, few colleges and universities train students in the languages of India. Even at centers of Indological research, popular trends in the humanities and social sciences often assume precedence over philology, palaeography, and manuscriptology. These educational trends are spreading to India as well. Neglect by scholars contributes to neglect by their custodians, resulting in peril to these valuable and unique artifacts of the heritage of India. The process of making critical editions is demanding and time consuming. The few scholars engaged in the process cannot possibly exhaust the work of collating all the extant manuscripts in critical editions within the remaining manuscript lifespan. Therefore the knowledge in manuscripts is in danger of perishing with its aging paper and palm-leaf substrates. Action must be taken to preserve this valuable knowledge and cultural heritage and to insure its accessibility in the new dominant medium of knowledge transmission.

1.3 Media transitions

The current transition of the dominant medium of knowledge transmission from printed book to electronic text is not the first transition in the medium of knowledge. History records two other such transitions: the transition from oral tradition to writing, and the transition from manuscript to printed text. The transition from oral tradition to writing is recorded in ancient Greece by Plato in the fifth century B.C.E. In Plato's *Phaedrus* (275a), for example, Socrates denigrates writing by relating the words of king Thamus of the Egyptian Thebes to the god Theuth when Theuth revealed the art of writing to him. When Theuth promised that it would make the people wiser and improve their memories, king Thamus retorts that it would have the very opposite effect. He says, "It will implant forgetfulness in their souls; they will cease to exercise memory because they rely on that which is written." While there are both benefits and detriments to the medium of writing vis à vis oral transmission, the passage recognizes the introduction of writing into disciplines of learning in Greece and recognizes Egyptian influence in this introduction.

Writing was introduced earlier, at the end of the fourth millenium B.C.E. in Sumeria and Egypt. The earliest documents record economic transactions such as the number of sheep sold or the numbers of bundles of grain collected in taxes. In India, while the Harrapan script remains undeciphered, the earliest extant uses of Kharoṣṭhī and Brāhmī scripts are on public monuments and in edicts. Aśoka commissioned the Brāhmī script for these administrative purposes during the expansion of his empire in the latter half of the third century B.C.E.

The introduction of writing was originally for administrative and economic purposes; it was not used initially for literary or scientific affairs. Only later did literary composition make the transition into the written medium. In India, the earliest inscriptions are in Prākrit, not in Sanskrit. The earliest Sanskrit inscriptions date to the first century B.C.E., two centuries later than the oldest inscription in Prakrit. The Vedic tradition and the core sūtra texts in Sanskrit continued to be transmitted orally millennia after Aśoka introduced writing for edicts in Prākrit even as writrng on paper and palm leaf became the principal means to distribute knowledge. Public performance also continued to be widely popular even as writing spread. Oral learning diminished gradually in educational systems around the world up to the present day. In India it remains alive only in Vedic pāthaśālas. In the West it has ceased even in language instruction and remains essential only in classes in the dramatic arts. Writing gradually crept from administrative into literary uses and overtook orality as the dominant mode of transmission in education.

Moveable type was invented by Gutenberg in 1445 C.E.. While the first typeface was used in a Latin textbook, it was very soon adopted for literary purposes. The Gutenberg Bible was printed just ten years later in 1455. Types were first employed in India to print Christian doctrine at a Jesuit printing press in Goa which operated between 1556 and 1674. Tamil types were created there in 1578. Devanāgarī types were first created in Rome in 1771 to print the *credo* in Hindi, and Charles Wilkins created a Devanāgarī typeface soon afterwards used to print his *A Grammar of the Sanskrita Language* in 1808. A Bengali grammar was printed in Hoogly in 1778. Printing gradually replaced manuscript copying as the dominant mode of knowledge transmission in India during the nineteenth and twentieth centuries. The first examples of printed typeface tended to imitate handwritten characters, and printers typecases, which counted hundreds of characters, included types for numerous ligatures. Characters were standardized and repertoires reduced to accomodate the restrictions of new technologies such as hot-metal typesetting and the typewriter.[1]

1.4 Preservation and loss of knowledge in media transitions

Knowledge exists fundamentally in the consciousness of knowledgeable people. They express and communicate that knowledge through speech, visual images, and performance and often combine these various means of communication. Oral communication is often accompanied by gestures, for instance. Each of these modes of communication has the potential to imitate the others. When a mode of communication is copied into another medium, the copy can be no better than its original. The copy selectively reproduces what the medium of reproduction permits and the copyist chooses to include. The transcription of a lecture will not include the gestures of the speaker nor his changes in intonation. In the same way, a manuscript reproduction of oral recitation of a Vedic text will lose much. Head and hand gestures and voice fluctuations will not be recorded. Yet special effort on the part of the copyist may

[1]For more detail, see Peter Scharf and Malcolm Hyman, Linguistic issues in encoding Sanskrit (Delhi: Motilal Banarsidass; Providence: The Sanskrit Library, 2011.)

extend the target medium to accomodate unusual information. The character set of ordinary written Sanskrit, for instance, was extended by marks used to capture pitch variation in Vedic. Yet if subsequent readers of the copy fail to understand the significance of certain marks, they will cease to understand what those marks represent in the original mode of communication. If no one remains to explain their significance that information will be lost. The significance of Vedic accent marks in less common traditions, such as in the Kāṭhaka and Maitrāyaṇī branches of Yajurveda, and Rāṇāyanīya and Jaiminīya branches of *Sāmaveda* for instance, is known to few and requires some research to discover. Roman transcriptions of these Vedic texts often obliterate the differences between different traditions of recitation.[2] The knowledge of these accentual traditions would perish with the death of a few individuals and the loss of a few volumes.

In general, knowledge gets lost in media transitions because a copy is no better than its original, the new medium cannot accomodate all the information present in the medium it copies, people fail to encode information accurately in the new medium, younger generations, accustomed to the new medium, cease to learn to access information in the old medium, and the substrate of the old medium perishes. Perserving knowledge in media transitions requires special attention to counter each of these points. It requires copying the most original form of the information, adapting the new medium to accommodate the desired information. creating methods to accurately encode desired information, adapting the presentation of old information to meet new standards of access, and timely action before the old medium perishes. Preserving knowledge in media transitions requires recognizing that the new medium is not a static inheritance. Intelligence, creativity, and effort can adapt the new medium to meet the needs of the information that is desired to be expressed.

---

[2]Peter Scharf, "Vedic accent: underlying versus surface." In *Devadattīyam: Johannes Bronkhorst Felititation Volume*, edited by François Voegeli et al. (Bern: Peter Lang, 2012 pp. 405–426.

New media provide technological advances that provide new possibilities for the propagation of knowledge. Writing endures for a considerable length of time while speech vanishes the moment after it is uttered. Printing allows the wide distribution of multiple exact copies with relatively little effort. Alphabetization is a technology appropriate to visual media such as writing and print. It allows one to locate sought items in a dictionary or index merely by the shared standard of the alphabetic order. Thesauri, typically memorized in oral medium, required much greater effort to learn; yet once learned allowed instant random access to their contents. Without the oral medium and memorization, they require much greater effort to access. Digital technology however delegates alphabetization to software and replaces manual use of alphabetized dictionaries and indices with the search interface. It allows random access without memorization. Recognizing the potential of the new medium and utilizing it to its fullest is essential for the preservation and propagation of knowledge. At the least, the expectations of users of the new medium of knowledge transmission need to be met lest information inaccessible by the methods to which they are accustomed simply gets disregarded, neglected, and lost.

1.5 Expectations regarding information access in the digital medium

Digital technology, computational linguistic methods, and the internet allow easier and faster access to information. Digital technology allows the magnification of text and images and enhancement of images through the adjustment of lighting and contrast. HTML interfaces permit greater synthesis and integration of information via linking than linear text in the printed or written medium does. The digital medium also allows information to be represented in various views without significant additional labor or expense. The digital medium allows easy access to greater detail and to obscure sources where access to physical copies would require prohibitive expense and effort.

Internet users expect to find what they are looking for on the web within seconds. Yet the seamless fulfillment of their expectations depends upon information processing technology that has developed primarily in the environment of the Roman alphabet. Functionality that is taken for granted for European languages has not yet been developed for other languages. One expects to be able to search a PDF file. One expects to be able to run optical character recognition (OCR) software on a PDF file to extract machine readable text. One expects to find material so extracted from PDF files in a general Web search interface. Generalized information extraction and search techniques cannot adequately handle literary materials for which there is a lack of adequate optical character recognition software, inconsistent encoding, obscure word boundaries, complex morphology, and free syntax. However the Sanskrit Library is developing just such tools for the principal culture-bearing language of India.

2. *Overcoming obstacles to access of Indian heritage*

The Sanskrit Library has and continues to develop the techniques and infrastructure necessary to integrate Sanskrit manuscripts embodying primary cultural heritage materials of India with digital text, lexical resources, and linguistic software. In a project funded by the U.S. National Science Foundation, the Sanskrit Library standardized Sanskrit text-encoding, revised the Unicode Standard to include characters necessary for Indic cultural heritage, supplied validated data for optical character recognition, prepared the major digital Sanskrit-English lexicon for integration with linguistic software, produced several other digital lexical resources, produced a full-form Sanskrit lexicon and morphological analyzer, and fostered international collaboration in the area of Sanskrit computational linguistics.

In their book *Linguistic issues in encoding Sanskrit,* Scharf and Hyman completed a comprehensive survey of linguistic and theoretical issues related to the encoding of Sanskrit language and designed accurate, principled phonetic encoding schemes for Sanskrit linguistic processing. Although Indic scripts reflect the phonetics of Sanskrit transparently, the orthography of the various semi-syllabic Brāhmī-based scripts of India departs from an ideal one-to-one coding of Sanskrit sounds. Yet the sophisticated linguistic traditions of India provide direct access to the phonology of the language thereby allowing the creation of encodings ideal for linguistic purposes. Three encodings: Sanskrit Library Phonetic basic (SLP1), which utilizes only ASCII codes, Sanskrit Library segmental (SLP2), which has a unique codepoint for each phonetic segment, regardless of accent, nasalization, length or other feature, and Sanskrit Library featural (SLP3), which encodes only the features that characterize sounds rather than phonetic segments.

After an investigation of Sanskrit paleography, Scharf initiated worldwide collaboration, including such partners as the Indian Ministry of Communications and Information Technology, the Centre for Development of Advanced Computing (C-DAC) in Mumbai, and the Script-encoding Initiative at Berkeley, to extend the Unicode Standard to include 68 additional characters required for the proper display of the ancient Vedic heritage texts of India. Unicode Standard version 5.2 incorporated the characters in two code blocks, Devanagari Extended and Vedic Extensions, both accessible under South Asian Scripts via the Unicode Character Code Charts page (<www.unicode.org/charts>).

The Sanskrit Library developed transcoding routines to translate between its phonetic encodings and standard and popular encodings used for data-entry and display. A preferences menu permits users to select desired input methods, such as Kyoto-Harvard, ITrans, Velthaus, WX, etc., and to display content in a variety of scripts including the major scripts of India, and standard Romanization.

By running our inflection software on the 170,000 nominal and verbal headwords in Monier-Williams', *A Sanskrit-English Dictionary* (Oxford: The Clarendon Press, 1899), the most complete English language dictionary of Sanskrit, we created a full-form lexicon of eleven million entries that associates each inflected form with its inflectional identifier and headword. The full-form lexicon allowed us to build a morphological analyzer. The analyzer displays all possible analyses of the inflected nominal form entered in the analyzer input field. Each analysis consists of the inflectional identifier and stem, the latter of which is a link to the Sanskrit Library multi-dictionary interface.

A current project jointly funded by the National Endowment for the Humanities (NEH) and the Deutsche Forschungsgemeinschaft (DFG) extends the Sanskrit Library's multi-dictionary interface by integrating supplements to the major bilingual dictionaries already included, and by adding specialized dictionaries, indigenous Indian monolingual dictionaries, traditional thesauri, and traditional linguistic analyses.

The Sanskrit Library obtained three hundred digital editions of texts from the Thesaurus Indogermanischer Text- und Sprachmaterialien at Johann Wolfgang Goethe Universität, Frankfurt am Main (<titus.uni-frankfurt.de>), the Vedic Reserve at Maharishi University of Management (<is 1.mum.edu/vedicreserve>), the NEH-funded grammatical databank project headed by George Cardona at the University of Pennsylvania in the early 1990's, and other sources, and displays them in a reader page. Each word in sandhi-analyzed texts dynamically links to the morphological analysis window where stems link to the multi-dictionary interface. This integration of digital texts, linguistic software, and lexical sources thus provides an environment in which users can easily access resources to assist in studying the texts they wish to read.

The Sanskrit Library texts additionally are integrated with Gérard Huet's Sanskrit Heritage Site parser using distributed interoperable Web services. In texts in which sandhi has not been analyzed, each sentence is a link to the Sanskrit Heritage Site parser (<sanskrit.inria.fr/DICO/reader.en.html>). The Sanskrit Heritage Site additionally allows one to submit compounds for further analysis by the compound analyzer built by Amba Kulkarni at the University of Hyderabad and to submit analyzed sentences for syntactic analysis by her dependency tree parser. Encouraged by the success of this sort of distributed international cooperation, Scharf, Huet, and Kulkarni collaborated with colleagues in forming the Sanskrit Computational Linguistics Consortium to hold symposia, workshops, and seminars to foster collaborative research and and resource sharing in Sanskrit natural language processing. Five symposia were held 2007–2013 in the U.S., France, and India with papers published by Springer and D. K. Printworld. [3]

In an NEH-funded project 2009–2012, entitled, "Enhancing Access to Primary Cultural Heritage Materials of India: Integrating images of literary sources with digital texts, lexical resources, linguistic software, and the web." the Sanskrit Library aimed to enhance access to primary cultural heritage materials of India housed in American libraries by integrating them with the digital texts, lexical resources, and linguistic software in the Sanskrit Library. The project developed protocols, formats, and software to integrate into its digital library digital images of 160 Sanskrit manuscripts, numbering 25,000 pages, that represent two central Indic texts, *Mahābhārata* and *Bhāgavata Purāṇa*, in the Brown University and University of Pennsylvania libraries. The project developed a comprehensive dynamic catalogue that allows access to manuscripts via numerous criteria and explored text-image alignment techniques to permit focused access to particular passages on manuscript pages by way of searching for the passage in corresponding digital text.

2.1 *Digital imaging*

Manuscript pages were photographed from above with daylight-balanced light fixtures illuminating the original from the left and right; images were captured with a default resolution of at least 300 dpi at

---

[3] *Sanskrit Computational Linguistics: First and Second International Symposia, Rocquencourt, France, October* 2007; *Providence, Rl, USA, May* 2008; *Revised Selected and Invited Papers*, ed. Gérard Huet, Amba Kulkarni, and Peter Scharf, Lecture Notes in Artificial Intelligence 5402 (Berlin-Heidelberg: Springer-Verlag, 2009). *Sanskrit Computational Linguistics: Third International Symposium, Hyderabad, India, January 2009, Proceedings*, ed. Gérard Huet, and Amba Kulkarni. Lecture Notes in Artificial Intelligence 5406 (Berlin; Heidelberg: Springer-Verlag, 2009). *Sanskrit Computational Linguistics: 4th International Symposium, New Delhi, India, December 2010, Proceedings*. ed. Girish Nath Jha. Lecture Notes in Artificial Intelligence 6465. Berlin; Heidelberg: Springer-Verlag, 2010. *Proceedings of the Fifth International Sanskrit Computational Linguistics Symposium* (*4–6 January 2013, IIT Bombay, Mumbai*) (New Delhi: D. K. Printworld, forthcoming).

a copy-stand using a Canon 1Ds Mark III camera fitted with a 50mm Zeiss lens. Archival master image data are stored in uncompressed TIFF files tagged with the sRGB IEC611966-2.1 colorspace profile and are converted to JPEG 2000 for web display.

In palm leaf manuscripts, each palm leaf was imaged individually with a color balancing measuring stick. In unbound paper manuscripts where leaves are often attached in pairs, pages were imaged in pairs, the verso of the first folio with the recto of the next. In order to allow more focused web display, paired JPEG images were split and all images cropped to within a few millimeters of their edges automatically using software developed by Donglai Wei for the project.

3. *Dynamic cataloguing*

3.1 Library catalogues

A typical library catalogue includes several categories of information regarding manuscripts. For example, the University of Pennsylvania's online catalogue Franklin includes the following categories:

1. title
2. description
   a. extent
   b. material
   c. dimensions
3. collection
4. notes
5. catalogue reference
6. language
7. script
8. notes

3.2 ACSAM data collection

The American Committee for South Asian Manuscripts (ACSAM) adopted much more thorough cataloguing standards. ACSAM was established by the late David Pingree in 1995 under the aegis of the American Oriental Society for the purpose of preserving and promoting access to the manuscripts of South Asia in North American collections. ACSAM prescribed the collection of data in twenty-three categories as shown below for the purpose of creating complete descriptive catalogue entries. These categories include explicit provision for bibliographic information of editions of the work and catalogues that mention the work, information about scribes, patrons and owners, the transcription of the beginning and end of the text, the closing (such as इति श्रीमद्भगवद्गीता समाप्ता called there 'colophon') and scribal trailers (called there 'post-colophon').

1. Collection
2. Shelf-mark
3. Foliation
4. Scribe's foliation
5. Lines
6. Dimensions
7. Material
8. Condition (e.g., tearing or other damage)
9. Binding
10. Script
11. Format
12. Commentary, glosses, notes
13. Incompleteness
14. Scribal hand changes
15. Scribe, place and date of copying, and person for whom
16. Owners
17. Bibliography
18. Gaps
19. Final colophon (author, title)
20. Post-colophon (scribe, place and date of copying)
21. Transcript of ownership and readership notes
22. Additional notes
23. Illustrations

3.3 The Sanskrit Library's TEI-Ms template

The "Enhancing Access to Primary Cultural Heritage Materials of India" project developed an XML manuscript cataloguing template in accordance with the guidelines of the Text Encoding Initiative's (TEI) Manuscript Description (<www.tei-c.org/release/doc/tei-p5-doc/en/html/MS.html>). The XML template incorporates the comprehensive standards of manuscript description and classification set by ACSAM. The categories included in the Sanskrit Library's manuscript cataloguing template are described below section by section while its complete structure is shown in Appendix A. In these descriptions nested element names are separated from the name of their parent by a dot and attributes are put in square brackets. The Text Encoding Initiative Manuscript Description guidelines allow for the complete transcription of a manuscript and a description of the encoded transcription in the TEI header element (teiHeader). The teiHeader element contains three subsections to describe the file, its encoding, and its categorization or profile:

1. fileDesc
2. encodingDesc
3. profileDesc

The fileDesc element includes an element for the description of the document source (sourceDesc) which in turn includes an element for the description of the manuscript (msDesc). The latter includes categories for the description of manuscript identifiers, manuscript contents, the physical condition of the manuscript, its history, and any additional information:

1. msIdentifier
2. msContents
3. physDesc
4. history
5. additional

Included in the TEI manuscript header's msIdentifier element are elements to designate the collection in which the manuscript is housed and its identifying number in that collection. Provision is also made for describing alternate identifiers which may describe the identification of the manuscript in catalogues:

1. collection
2. idno
3. altIdentifier[type='catalog'].collection
4. altIdentifier[type='catalog'].idno

Included in the TEI manuscript header's msContents element is an msItem or msItemStruct element that describes the content of a work or a part of a work. The element may be repeated for each work contained in a manuscript and may be nested to describe sections or subsections of a work. Figure 1 shows the first half of the msItemStruct element of UPenn 490 containing the *Bhīṣmastavarāja*. The msItem and msItemStruct elements contain an indication of whether the manuscript is complete or not, and elements to describe the author, title, headings (rubric), beginning of the work proper (incipit), end of the work proper (explicit), its closing (here called 'finalRubric') scribal trailer (here called 'colophon'), and its language and script. The note element includes elements to mark names of people, titles, bibliographic information, etc. While the msItem element allows freer structuring and repetition of elements, the msItemstruct preserves information included in the following order for simpler automated processing:

1. msItemStruct[defective='truelfalse']
2. author
3. title
4. rubric
5. incipit
6. explicit
7. finalRubric

8. colophon
9. note
    a. persName
    b. title
    c. bibl
10. textLang[mainLang='ll-Ssss']

The physDesc element includes elements to describe the physical aspects of the manuscript including the type of object (folia or codex), its material basis (supportDesc), arrangement of the text on each page (layoutDesc), a description of the scribal hands (handDesc), decorations (decoDesc), interlinear and marginal notes and corrections (additions), the binding (bindingDesc), seal (sealDesc), and any accompanying matter such as letters of donation or acquisition forms (accMat):

1. objectDesc[form='folialcodex']
    a. supportDesc
    b. layoutDesc
2. handDesc
3. decoDesc
4. additions
5. bindingDesc
6. sealDesc.seal
7. accMat

Description of the material basis (supportDesc) includes elements that describe the material (paper or palm leaf), size and quantity of leaves, their enumeration (foliation), and collation (these latter two including regular formulae amenable to digital processing), abbreviated titles that accompany enumeration (signatures), and the condition of the material basis.

1. support.material
2. extent.measure
3. extent.dimensions

4. foliation
5. foliation.formula
6. foliation.signatures
7. collation
8. collation.formula
9. condition

```
<msContents>
 <msItemStruct defective='false'>
  <locus from='1r' to='17v' target='#images'>ff. 1r--17v</locus>
  <author xml:lang='sa-Latn-x-SLP1'>{k}fzRa {d}vEpAyana {v}yAsa</author>
  <title type='main' xml:lang='sa-Latn-x-SLP1'
      rend='bold'>{B}IzmastavarAja</title>
  <title type='context' xml:lang='sa-Latn-x-SLP1'
      rend='bold'>{m}ahABArata</title>
  <title type='context' xml:lang='sa-Latn-x-SLP1'
      rend='bold'>{S}Antiparvan</title>
  <incipit xml:lang='sa-Latn-x-SLP1' corresp='#sp1'>
   <locus from='1v' facs='#f1v' xml:lang='en'>f. 1v</locus>
  </incipit>
  <explicit xml:lang='sa-Latn-x-SLP1' corresp='#v127'>
   <locus from='17r' facs='#f17r' xml:lang='en'>f. 17r</locus>
  </explicit>
  <finalRubric xml:lang='sa-Latn-x-SLP1' corresp='#fr'>
   <locus from='17r' to='17v' facs='#f17r #f17v' xml:lang='en'>f. 17r--f.
       17v</locus>
  </finalRubric>
  <colophon>none</colophon>
  <note xml:id='BhSRdesc'>The concluding verse <ref
      target='#v127'>127</ref> on <locus from='17r' facs='#f17r'>f.
      17r</locus>, <q>Finished is this sin-destroying regal praise of
      <persName type='character'
      xml:lang='sa-Latn-x-SLP1'>{v}izRu</persName> of wonderful deeds
      previously sung by the son of the Ganges (<persName type='character'
      xml:lang='sa-Latn-x-SLP1'>{B}Izma</persName>)</q>, and the <ref
      target='#fr'>final rubric</ref> on <locus from='17v' facs='#f17v'>f.
      17v</locus>, <q>Finished is the regal hymn of praise uttered by
      <persName type='character'
      xml:lang='sa-Latn-x-SLP1'>{B}Izma</persName> in the <title
      type='mentioned' xml:lang='sa-Latn-x-SLP1'
      rend='italic'>{r}AjaDarma</title> section in the <title
      type='mentioned' xml:lang='sa-Latn-x-SLP1'
      rend='italic'>{S}Antiparvan</title> in the <title type='mentioned'
      xml:lang='sa-Latn-x-SLP1' rend='italic'>{m}ahABArata</title> of a
      hundred thousand verses</q>, identify the text as the <title
      type='mentioned' xml:lang='sa-Latn-x-SLP1'
      rend='italic'>{B}IzmastavarAja</title>, which comprises the contents
```

Fig. 1. Image showing a partial view of the msContents element in the Sanskrit Library manuscript catalogue XML file for UPenn 490.

Description of the layout indicates how many columns and lines are on each page and anything else that may describe the layout of the text. For example, the layout element may describe that a base text is indented flanked above and below by commentary in an hourglass arrangement. The layoutDesc element includes the following elements for this purpose:

1. layout
2. layout[columns]
3. layout[writtenLines]

The handDesc element includes an element to summarize the scribal hands, if necessary as well as a repeatable element to describe the handwriting of each scribe:

1. summary
2. handNote

Description of the decoration is done by the use of decoNote elements provided with various values of a type attribute to distinguish description of colors, borders, illustrations, and diagrams:

1. decoNote[type='color']
2. decoNote[type='border']
3. decoNote[type='illustration']
4. decoNote[type='diagram'

The bindingDesc element lets one indicate whether there is a binding, what sort of binding it is, the materials it uses, and its condition:

1. binding
2. condition

The TEI manuscript header's history element includes elements to describe the origin of the manuscript as well as facts about its subsequent locations, ownership and use (provenance). Elements are provided to mark the date when it was completed. (origDate), the names of the scribe, patron, and owner (persName), the place of origin (placeName, geogName). These name elements may also be used to describe details of the manuscripts provenance, and its acquisition by the current repository.

1. origin
   a. origDate
   b. persName type='scribelowner'
   c. placeName
   d. geogName
2. provenance
3. acquisition

The TEI manuscript file description closes with the additional element which includes within a record history element (recordHist) subsumed under an administrative information element (adminInfo) elements that describe the source of the infomation that is included in the XML catalogue record itself and any changes made to that record:

1. source
2. change

The encodingDesc element defines the term of reference to the Library of Congress Subject Headings, and provides a definition of symbols used in the standard classification of Sanskrit metrical patterns. The profileDesc element includes elements in which to list Library of Congress Subject Headings that describe the manuscript, and to classify the manuscript in accordance with the Sanskrit Library's own Indic subject classification. The latter, shown in Appendix B, is based upon well-known traditional divisions of disciplines. The manuscripts of the *Bhāgavata Purāṇa* for instance are classified as Purāṇa. The classification of the manuscripts of parts of the *Mahābhārata* subsumes them under the category Itihāsa.

3.4 *Facsimiles*

The software developed by Donglai Wei to split and crop images (see section 2.1) also produced an XML file containing references to the images and their cropped zones in accordance with the TEI guidelines. Ralph Bunker, the technical director of the Sanskrit Library and software engineer for the NEH project, developed software to assign descriptive names to each page image in conformity with the foliation element in the teiHeader manuscript description. While manuscript photographers assign names in sequence such as UPenn490_0001, UPenn490_0002, etc., descriptive names refer to the folio and side, such as 'f. 1r' for the recto of the first folio. Anomalies occur in the association of a directory of the images of a manuscript with the enumeration of leaves in the foliation element when for example the directory of images includes images of accompanying documents and bindings which are not included in the foliation element. Anomalies also occur when duplicate images are delivered or when pages are inadvertently skipped. Bunker developed the Folio software to compare image references with directory contents and generate a report of misalignments. Folio then produces an HTML display that allows human validation of image references by comparison with miniature images and with page references in annotations produced by the SITA software described below (see Figure 11). Cataloguers adjust misaligned names by editing an XML pages directory to indicate anomalies. Once references are validated, Bunker's catalogue preparation software inserts the TEI graphic references with their descriptive narne identifiers into the facsimiles element in the TEI manuscript catalogue entry file.

3.5 *Transcription*

Transcription is made just once in the body of a document. The Sanskrit Library TEI manuscript catalogue entry files place all transcriptions of manuscript contents, such as rubrics, incipits, explicits, final rubrics, and colophons. solely in the text element in the body of the TEI document. Elements are used there to indicate text divisions (div). headings (head) and closings (trailer), speeches (sp), the introduction of speakers (speaker), verses (1g) and lines of verse (l), paragraphs (p), sentences (s), other segments of text such as verse quarters or sections of paragraphs or trailers (seg), gaps in the manuscript (gap), and bibliography corresponding to transcribed passages (bibl):

1. div
2. head
3. trailer
4. sp.speaker
5. lg
6. l
7. seg
8. p
9. s
10. gap reason='missing|damage|partialTranscript'
11. bibl

These text markup elements may be supplied with XML identifier attributes (xml:id) that permit them to be the target of reference. Elements that describe the textual contents of each work in the msContents element of the TEI header (rubric, incipit, explicit, finalRubric, and colophon) make formal reference to the relevant textual elements by the use of the corresp attribute. Bibliographic references from identified passages in published works many include corresp attributes that refer to the passage in a digital edition of the text.

The extensive markup available for use in the Sanskrit Library manuscript catalogue template just described allows catalogue entries to be indexed by numerous criteria in order to provide an extremely versatile catalogue index interface. It is not necessary, however, that all these details be provided for every manuscript in order to include the entry in the catalogue and to produce a handsome display of the catalogue entry. The Sanskrit Library developed software to format whatever information is provided automatically in an HTML display and to include that information automatically in a dynamic catalogue index.

3.6 The Sanskrit Library manuscript catalogue HTML display

The Sanskrit Library Siva software generates HTML pages from the TEI XML catalogue entry files. The software neatly formats the catalogue data, graphic references, and text in the XML file and automatically generates hyperlinks. Figure 2 shows the HTML display of the contents of the manuscript UPenn 490 produced from the TEI XML source file shown in Figure 1. Links lead from notes in the catalogue description to transcribed passages, from XML graphic references in the facsimiles section to digital images, from title abbreviations to full bibliographic descriptions, and from bibliographic scope references to corresponding digital texts and annotated manuscript images. For example clicking on the verse number 127 in the beginning of the note in Figure 2 scrolls to the transcription section to show verse 127 of the *Bhīṣmastavarāja* in context. Clicking the manuscript page

Contents

Work 1 (complete)

Locus: ff. 1r–17v
Author: Kṛṣṇa Dvaipāyana Vyāsa
Title: **Bhīṣmastavarāja**
Incipit: f. 1v
.. janamejaya uvāca .. ..
śaratalpe śayānas tu bhāratānāṁ pitāmahaḥ
katham utsṛṣṭavān deham kaṁ cid yogam adhārayat ..1.. (Anuṣṭubh) (MBh. 12.47.1)
Explicit: f. 17r
stavarājaḥ samāpto yaṁ viṣṇor adbhutakarmaṇaḥ
gāṁgeyena purā gīto mahāpātakanāśanaḥ ..127.. (MBh. 12.47.65*98, lines 3–4) (Anuṣṭubh)
Final rubric: f. 17r–f. 17v
iti śrīmahābhārate satasahasryāṁ saṁhitāyāṁ śāṁtiparvaṇi rājadharme bhīṣmoktaṁ stavarājastotraṁ saṁpūrṇam ..
Colophon: none
Note: The concluding verse 127 on f. 17r, 'Finished is this sin-destroying regal praise of Viṣṇu of wonderful deeds previously sung by the son of the Ganges (Bhīṣma)', and the final rubric on f. 17v, 'Finished is the regal hymn of praise uttered by Bhīṣma in the *Rājadharma* section in the *Śāntiparvan* in the *Mahābhārata* of a hundred thousand verses', identify the text as the *Bhīṣmastavarāja*, which comprises the contents of Adhyāya 47 in the *Rājadharma* section of the *Śāntiparvan* of the *Mahbharata* (MBh. 12.47.1–12.47.72). Bhīṣma sings this praise of Viṣṇu just prior to abandoning his arrow-filled body. The manuscript is 75% longer than the text in the Pune critical edition. The last two verses of the text (MBh. 12.47.71–72) in the critical edition correspond with verses 119–120 on f. 16r of the ms., though the latter varies considerably. While the text of the chapter in the critical edition ends there, the ms. continues with six additional verses, four of which correspond with verses in the star passages in the critical apparatus: verse 121 on f. 16r corresponds with the first two lines of star passage 98 inserted by M1.3 after MBh. 12.47.65 while the concluding verse 127 on f. 17r corresponds with lines three and four of star passage 98. Verse 122 on f. 16v corresponds with lines 5–8 of star passage 94 inserted by K4 and Dn after MBh. 12.47.60, verse 124 on f. 16v corresponds with lines 5–8 of star passage 99 inserted by D7, T, and G1.2 after MBh. 12.47.72, and verse 125 on f. 16v–f. 17r corresponds with lines 1–4 of the same passage. Verses 123 (in Anuṣṭubh meter) and 126 (in Mālinī meter) are not found in the critical text or apparatus.
Language: Sanskrit in Devanāgarī script

Fig. 2. Image showing a partial view of the contents section in the Sanskrit Library manuscript catalogue HTML file for UPenn 490.

reference f.17r in the same note, opens an image of the recto of folio 17. The link to this image is also found listed in order in the facsimiles section, and in the manuscript view of the transcription section. Clicking the title abbreviation *MBh.* in the bibliographic reference at the end of the incipit in the content section shown in Figure 2 displays a bibliographic description of the Pune critical edition of the *Mahābhārata*. Finally, clicking the bibliographic scope reference 12.47.1 (parvan, adhyāya, and verse numbers) at the end of the bibliographic reference in the incipit opens the alignment display interface shown in Figure 12. Figure 12 displays the text of the Sanskrit Library's digital edition of the *Sāntiparvan* of the *Mahābhārata*, which contains the *Bhīṣmastavarāja*, scrolled to the beginning of the *Bhīṣmastavarāja*. The alignment display interface is described further below in section 4.

Text in the Sanskrit Library manuscript catalogue HTML display is displayed in the transcription section in two layouts. Initially the text is displayed in text layout in accordance with the structure of the text as shown in Figure 3. Verses are formatted in metrical lines and pādas. Each sentence of prose is put on a separate line, as are headings and trailers, and bibliographic references are shown. Editorial corrections, notes and references are displayed. Clicking the "Show manuscript layout" button displays the transcription in accordance with the page and line structure of the manuscript itself as shown in Figure 4. Each line in the manuscript is displayed on its own line and the lines on a page are displayed beneath the folio number of that page. References, notes, and corrections are removed to avoid interrupting the original layout.

The folio page reference in the manuscript layout is a link to the image of that page. For instance, clicking f.1v in Figure 4 opens an image of the verso of folio 1. As in bibliographic references in the content section described above, in the text structure layout too, the abbreviation of the title (*MBh.* after verse 1 in Figure 3) is a link to the full bibliographic description, and the bibliographic scope reference links to the corresponding digital text displayed in the alignment display interface. For example, clicking 12.41.1 at the end

Show manuscript layout

Transcription (text structure)

śrīgaṇeśāya namaḥ ..
.. janamejaya uvāca .. ..
śaratalpe śayānas tu bhāratānāṁ pitāmahaḥ
katham utsṛṣṭavān dehaṁ kaṁ cid yogam adhārayat ..1.. (Anuṣṭubh) (MBh. 12.47.1)
vaiśaṁpāyana uvāca ..
śṛṇuṣvāvahito rājan śucir bhūtvā samāhitaḥ
bhīṣmas tu kuruśārdūla dehotsargaṁ samāśrayat 2 (MBh. 12.47.2) (Anuṣṭubh)
<..>
<..>
<..> (Anuṣṭubh)
śrībhīṣma uvāca ..
ārādhayāmy ahaṁ viṣṇuṁ vācaṁ jigadiṣāmy ahaṁ
tayā vyāsasamāsīnyā prīyatāṁ puruṣottamaḥ 13 (MBh. 12.47.10) (Anuṣṭubh)

Fig. 3. Image showing a partial view of the text structure layout in the Sanskrit Library manuscript catalogue HTML file for UPenn 490.

of the bibliographic reference in Figure 3 opens the alignment display interface shown in Figure 12.

3.7 The Sanskrit Library manuscript catalogue index

The Sanskrit Library manuscript catalogue index provides numerous avenues to locate manuscripts. These avenues are not limited just to the ordinary criteria of author, title, institution, manuscript identifiers, language, script and subject heading found in most library and manuscript catalogues, though these categories are also available in the initially displayed general pane of the index. The numerous categorical, keyword, and text searches the index provides go much further than just allowing one to locate known texts and manuscripts. They also provide a research tool to gather information about various aspects of manuscript culture ranging from the content of works and historical information to scribal practices and material culture.

The identifiers pane permits not just a detailed search by catalogues that mention the manuscript as well as by the housing collection and its identifier. It includes in addition menus to search

Show text structure

Transcription (manuscript layout)

f.1v
Line 1: śrīgaṇeśāya namaḥ .. .. janamejaya uvāca .. .. śarata
Line 2: lpe śayānas tu bhāratānāṁ pitāmahaḥ katham utsṛṣṭavān de
Line 3: haṁ kaṁ cid yogam adhārayat ..1.. vaiśaṁpāyana uvāca .. śṛṇu
Line 4: ṣvāvahito rājan śucir bhūtvā samāhitaḥ bhīṣmas tu ku
Line 5: ruśārdūla dehotsargaṁ samāśrayat 2 <..> <..>

f.3r
Line 1: <..> śrībhīṣma uvāca ..
Line 2: ārādhayāmy ahaṁ viṣṇuṁ vācaṁ jigadiṣāmy ahaṁ tayā
Line 3: vyāsasamāsīnyā prīyatāṁ puruṣottamaḥ 13 <..>

f.15r
Line 2: <..> iti vidyātapoyonir ayonir viṣṇur ī
Line 3: ḍitaḥ vāgyajñenārcito devaḥ prīyatāṁ me janārddanaḥ ..11..
Line 4: vaiśaṁpāyana uvāca .. etāvad uktvā vacanaṁ bhīṣmas tadgata
Line 5: mānasaḥ namaskṛtyaiva kṛṣṇāya prayāṇam akarot tadā 12 <..>

Fig. 4. Image showing a partial view of the manuscript layout in the Sanskrit Library manuscript catalogue HTML file for UPenn 490.

by the city ('settlement'), institution, and repository separately in case the precise identifiers are not known.

The person and title panes include menus to search by various categories besides the usual author and title, the latter of which finds whatever particular title the housing library chose to give the manuscript. Hence one can search by the name of an author or editor of a work mentioned in the catalogue description who is not necessarily the author or editor of the work included in the manuscript. One can search by characters that participate in a work thereby allowing one to locate works regarding a theme of interest regardless of the title of the work. For example, one can search for Bhīṣma or Yudhiṣṭhira to locate works in which these characters participate. Or one can search for Hāhā or Hūhū to discover that the

Gajendramokṣaṇa narrates the tale of how these two vying celestial musicians were cursed by the competition judge, whose judgement was doubted, to be born as a crocodile and elephant. The ability to search for the names of scribes, owners or any other persons permits one to research the prosopography of a person mentioned in a different context. The ability to search for date of origin, and place of origin or provenance in the history pane offers similar facility.

The content pane (shown in Figure 5) allows one to search for a particular passage that occurs in a rubric, incipit, explicit, final rubric, colophon or addition. One can also search for the abbreviated titles that accompany enumeration (signatures). One can search for manuscripts in the description of which certain Sanskrit terms have been used or in which the meter of transcribed verses has been identified. These search avenues may assist scholars in identifying the content of other manuscripts as well as in finding manuscripts in the Sanskrit Library. For example, if one is attempting to identify the work in a manuscript for which no title or final rubric is available but which has ना written above the number on the verso of each folio, one can select ना from the signature menu on the content pane in the Sanskrit Library manuscript catalogue index, click the submit button to find that UPenn 2639 contains such a signature,

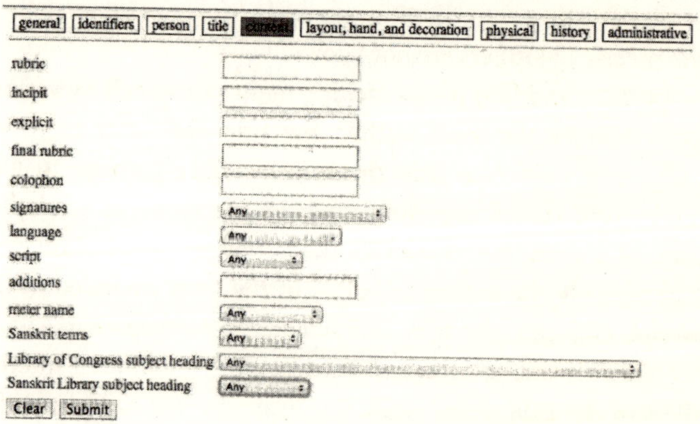

Fig. 5. Image showing the content pane in the Sanskrit Library manuscript catalogue index.

click the link penn2639.html listed below to open its HTML catalogue entry, scroll down to the physical description section, note under the signatures label that ना is similarly used in work 5 of this manuscript, scroll up to the content section and discover in the description of work 5 that it is titled *Nāgalīlā*. If one were unable to identify the work in a manuscript missing its first and last pages whose second folio began मया हि देव, one could search for the passage in the incipit's text box on the content pane of the Sanskrit Library manuscript catalogue index and quickly locate five manuscripts of the *Gajendramokṣaṇa* that begin with these words.

The layout, hand, and decoration pane allows one to search for manuscripts by the number of lines, colors. certain keywords used to describe different hands and border decorations, as well as to search for illustrations. One can select, for instance, the illustration description that begins, "The ms. contains five full-color illustrations," to locate UPenn Ms. Indic 5 (see Figure 6). click the link msindic5.html to open its HTML catalogue entry, scroll down to the decoration section, read the descriptions of the illustrations there (see Figure 7), and click on the folio link f.206v to open the manuscript page accompanying the narration of the *Gajendramokṣaṇa* that shows the illustration of Viṣṇu accompanied by Garuḍa liberating the elephant from the crocodile in the lake (see Figure 8).

The physical pane allows one to search by the type ofobject (codex or folia), material (various types of paper or palm leaf), number of leaves, height and width, collation (single or paired leaves), and

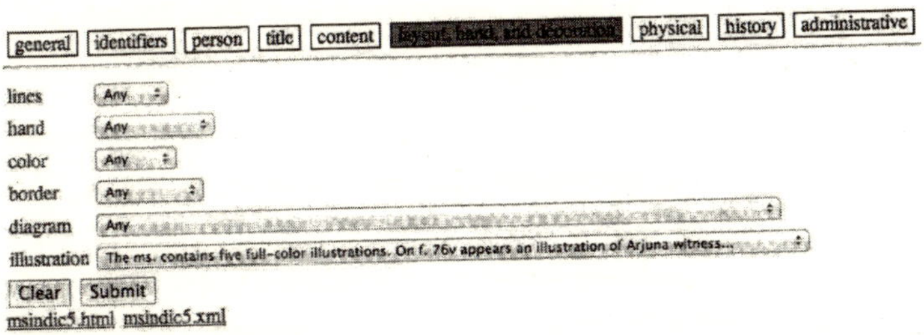

Fig. 6. Image showing the layout, hand, and decoration pane in the Sanskrit Library manuscript catalogue index.

Illustration: The ms. contains five full-color illustrations. On (modern foliation scheme) f. 76v appears an illustration of Arjuna witnessing Viṣṇu's four-armed form seated on a lotus holding a lotus, beads, and conch, with the heads of Gaṇeśa, Brahmā, himself, Śiva, and others surrounding his head.

On (modern foliation scheme) f. 130v appears an illustration of Viṣṇu reclining on Śeṣa with Lakṣmī sitting before him, Brahmā sitting in a lotus emerging from his navel, and Śiva to Brahmā's right in the background.

On (modern foliation scheme) f. 164v appears an illustration of Kṛṣṇa in Viṣṇu's four-armed form holding beads, a lotus, and conch attending Bhīṣma lying on his bed of arrows with Arjuna firing arrows into his mattress.

On (modern foliation scheme) f. 190v appears an illustrated elderly man on a couch with a pillow holding beads (perhaps Śaunaka) addressing a younger man sitting on the floor with a pillow (perhaps Śatānīka) in a palace.

On (modern foliation scheme) f. 206v appears an illustration of Viṣṇu accompanied by Garuḍa liberating the elephant from the crocodile in the lake.

Fig. 7. Image showing the description of illustrations in the decoration section in the Sanskrit Library manuscript catalogue HTML file for UPenn 490.

Fig. 8. Image showing the illustration, accompanying the narration of the *Gajendramokṣaṇa*, of Viṣṇu accompanied by Garuḍa liberating the elephant from the crocodile in the lake. The painting appears on f. 206v of UPenn Ms. Indic 5.

certain keywords describing the condition, binding, binding material and seal. Finally, the administrative pane allow one to search by the entry editor and the date of last revision.

The dynamic catalogue software generates the index from an XML driver file (index.xml) that describes the categories to be shown, and how they are grouped in various panes and lists the paths to the XML elements that contain the relevant information in the Sanskrit

Library XML manuscript catalogue entry files. The catalogue index can thus be revised or restructured without reprogramming just by editing the XML drive file.

4. *Text-image alignment*

The Sanskrit Library developed the Sanskrit image-text alignment interface (SITA) to facilitate human alignment of digital images of manuscript pages with the corresponding digital text. Search and display software utilizes the alignment to provide dynamic direct access to individual manuscript pages that contain passages specifically sought.

The context that contains the sought passage, which was aligned previously with digital text using the SITA software, is shown demarcated in each manuscript page image. Facilities to search for digital text is thus extended to digital manuscript images. This extension allows generalized information extraction and search techniques to reach Sanskrit manuscripts. The text-image alignment also allows a scholar viewing a manuscript immediate access to the digital analytic tools developed by the Sanskrit Library and its partners in the International Sanskrit Computational Linguistics Consortium such as a parser, morphological analyzer, and digital dictionaries.

In the course of the three-year NEH-funded manuscript project, an assistant familiar with Devanāgarī and Telugu scripts and experienced in working with manuscripts used the SITA software to align some 25,000 manuscript pages with their corresponding digital texts. The SITA software displays an image of one or two manuscript pages on the left, the corresponding digital text on the right, and a comment box on the lower right. Figure 9 shows an example from UPenn 490, a paper manuscript of the *Bhīṣmastavarāja*. At the left is displayed an image of the verso of folio 1 and the recto of folio 2 of the manuscript. A section of text on the recto of folio 1 marked at its beginning and end by small red brackets is correlated with a selection of digital text highlighted in grey on the right. The selection (MBh. 12.47.1–3) is the opening of the *Bhīṣmastavarāja* (the praise of

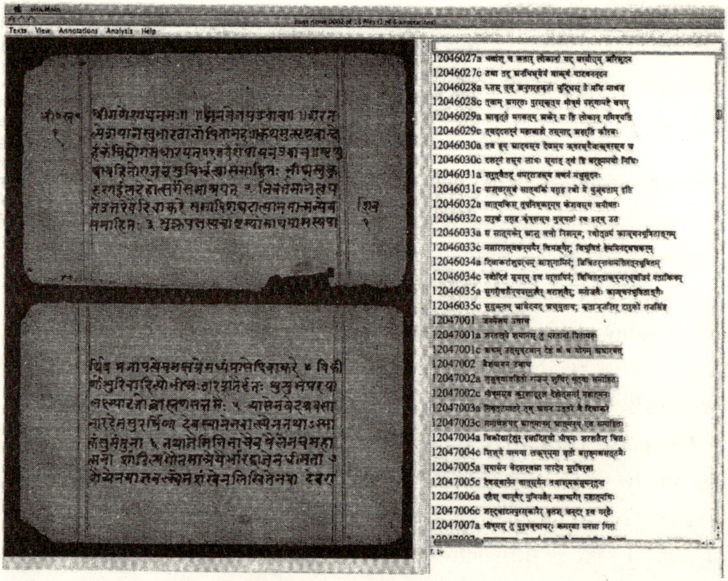

Fig. 9. Annotation of an image of f. lv–2r of UPenn Ms. Coll. 390, Item 490 in the Sanskrit image-text alignment software (SITA). The passage demarcated in red brackets on f. lv is aligned with *MBh.* 12.47.1–3, the beginning of the *Bhīṣmastavarāja* in the *Sāntiparvan* of the *Mahābhārata*, and the folio reference is provided in the comment box at the lower right.

Viṣṇu by Bhīṣma) which occurs in the twelfth book (*parvan*) of the *Mahābhārata*. In the comment box at the lower right, the page on which the annotated passage occurs is written. The text in red in the manuscript image that precedes the open bracket is an invocation not included in the digital edition. It is identified as a benediction in the comment box in another annotation while no text is selected in the digital edition.

Figure 10 shows an XML file of the SITA text-image alignment and annotation records. The first and last annotation elements record the annotations described in the previous paragraph. The attributes x1, y1 and x2, y2 record the coordinates of the marks in the image. The attributes start and end in the first annotation element record the beginning and end of the selection in the digital text. The bracketed CDATA contains the comments recording the page number 'f. lv' in

```
<annotations page='MBh12ShantiParvan/UPenn/mscoll390_item490' width='890'
    pc='-65536'>¬
Δ   <annotation type='sf' x1='1298' y1='465' x2='921' y2='1290' start='163010'
        end='163355' ><![CDATA[f. 1v]]></annotation>¬
Δ   <annotation type='sf' x1='2128' y1='2115' x2='1062' y2='2733'
        start='163356' end='163556' ><![CDATA[f. 2r]]></annotation>¬
Δ   <annotation type='sf' x1='946' y1='1195' x2='2298' y2='1265'
        ><![CDATA[passage is in manuscript but not in digital
        text]]></annotation>¬
Δ   <annotation type='sf' x1='564' y1='2120' x2='2111' y2='2223'
        ><![CDATA[passage is in manuscript but not in digital
        text]]></annotation>¬
Δ   <annotation type='sf' x1='1078' y1='2630' x2='2285' y2='2945'
        ><![CDATA[passage is in manuscript but not in digital
        text]]></annotation>¬
Δ   <annotation type='sf' x1='568' y1='465' x2='1240' y2='560'
        ><![CDATA[benediction]]></annotation>¬
</annotations>¬
```


Fig. 10. XML data file containing annotations of f. 1v-2r of UPenn Ms. Coll. 390, Item 490 produced with the Sanskrit image-text alignment software (SITA). The annotation elements may contain attributes x1, y1, x2, y2 indicating the coordinates of the open and close brackets demarcating a passage in the image, attributes start and end indicating the beginning and end of the corresponding passage in the digital text, and CDATA containing a comment.

the first annotation and the comment 'benediction' in the last. The comment 'benediction' is one item in a list of standard comments made available to the annotater and expanded as warranted in the course of the project. These comments also identify rubrics, final rubrics, colophons, text written at unusual angles, missing or additional passages, marginal additions, corrections, and bindings. The list of standard comments is shown in Table 1.

The page number in annotations supplies a check against the automated alignment produced from the foliation element of the manuscript catalogue entry in the page reference validation interface produced by the Folio software shown in Figure 11. Highlighted in red are shown the filename of the original image, the page numbers predicted by the foliation formula, and page numbers indicated in SITA annotations. Miniatures of the original image and the split and cropped images are displayed at the right. The interface allows a reviewer to check the correspondence quickly. Here the page numbers correspond, but the cropped images are in reverse order.

comment
Ask Dr. Scharf about this
rubric
final rubric
colophon
benediction
this is commentary
text is written vertically up the right margin
text is written vertically down the right margin
text is written vertically up the left margin
text is written vertically down the left margin
passage is in manuscript but not in digital text
passage is in digital text but not in manuscript
marginal addition in the same hand to be inserted at insertion point
marginal addition in a different hand to be inserted at insertion point
marginal correction in the same hand
marginal correction in a different hand
deletion of text painted over in yellow pigment
missing text indicated by an ellipsis mark
part of the folio containing text is missing
one blank page
two blank pages
variant
misordered image file
misordered manuscript leaf
inverted manuscript image
front cover
inside front cover
back cover
inside back cover

Table 1. Sanskrit image-text alignment standard comments

The discovery of randomly ordered cropped images led to revision of the splitting software to constrain zone ordering based upon the zones' y-coordinates.

5. Integrated digital access to inherited knowledge

The XML annotation records created in SITA allow multiple manuscript images to be linked to searchable digital texts thereby

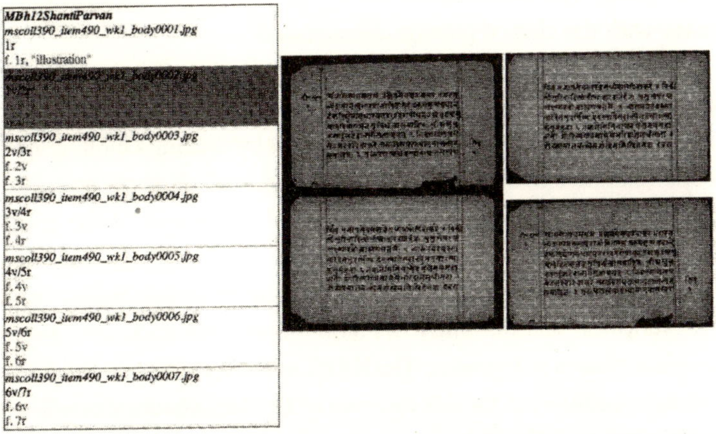

Fig. 11. The Sanskrit Library Folio interface used to validate references to manuscript pages in image files. Highlighted in red at the left are the file name of the original image, pages predicted by the catalogue entry's foliation formula, and page numbers inserted in the comment box of the SITA software. The original image, and split and cropped images are shown at the right, the latter erroneously in inverse order here.

allowing focused access to individual pages in manuscript images that contain the sought passage. The text-image alignmemt annotations created in SITA and written to XML files were used to create the Sanskrit image-text alignment display interface that links digital text passages to the digital images showing corresponding passages demarcated with red angle brackets in each manuscript. The alignment display interface displays the digital text. While the current display is in standard Romanization, it can be displayed in the other scripts included in the Sanskrit Library's transcoding software described above in section 2. A menu in the top left corner of the interface lists all the manuscripts that contain text corresponding to the digital text. The text the selected manuscript contains is highlighted in yellow while text it does not contain appears in white. Clicking a yellow passage in the digital text displays the manuscript image that contains the corresponding passage with the passage demarcated with red angle brackets. The passage in the digital text is colored green, and additional text contained in other annotations in the image appears in blue. Clicking the blue shows the manuscript image with the clicked passage demarcated.

The Sanskrit image-text alignment display interface is accessible from the catalogue entries of particular manuscripts as well as from the Sanskrit Library's text catalogue. Access by clicking a bibliographic scope reference in a catalogue entry was described above in section 3.6. Clicking the scope reference 12.47.1 at the end of the incipit in the manuscript contents description of UPenn 490 shown in Figure 2, or at the end of verse 1 in the verse structure display in the transcription section shown in Figure 3 opens the alignment display interface shown in Figure 12. The HTML interface contains the text of the digital edition of the *Sāntiparvan* of the *Mahābhārata* scrolled to the beginning of the *Bhīṣmastavarāja*. The incipit of the text is shown in green, and the manuscript image with the corresponding passage demarcated is displayed below it. By selecting other manuscripts from the menu in the upper left corner, the corresponding passage in those manuscripts is displayed. A search box at the top of the page allows one to search for other passages in that text.

One may also access the Sanskrit image-text alignment display interface by searching for a passage in the Sanskrit Library text window. For example, searching for *sadasad* opens the alignment display interface with the passage located in the first manuscript in which it is found. Selecting UPenn 490 from the menu displays the passage in that manuscript as shown in Figure 13.

The comments in annotations made in SITA allow one to locate annotations of a particular type, or annotations whose comments contain a particular term. Searching for these comments provides access to a number of interesting features of manuscripts. An interface will soon be built to provide access to manuscript images via the list of standard comments shown in Table 1 or by search of the text comments contain. At the present, they are searchable by a text editor.

6. Sharing expertise for the propagation of knowledge and culture

Digital technology is flexible. This flexibility allows incremental development of software as well as progressive addition of data.

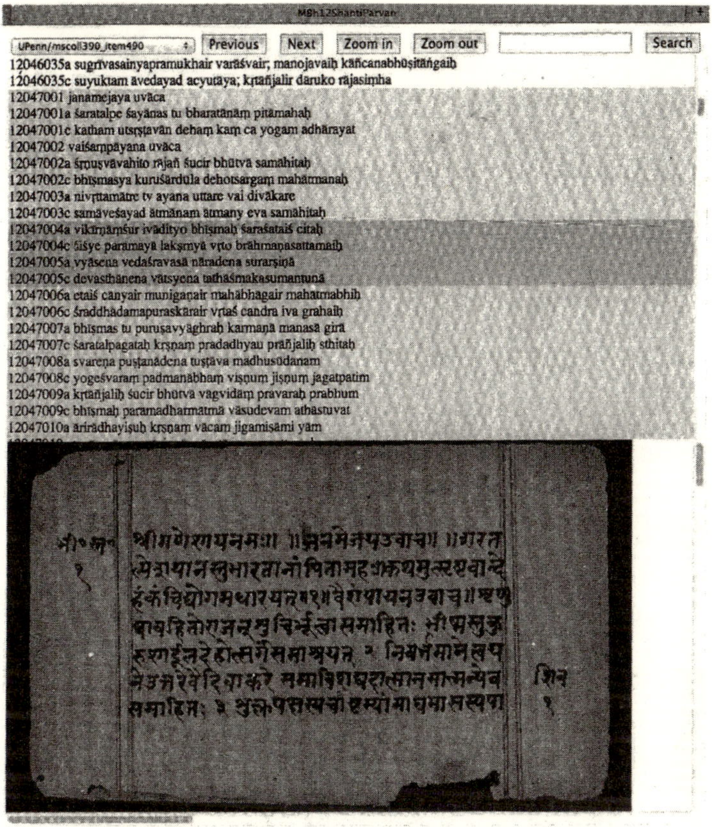

Fig. 12. Image showing the Sanskrit image-text alignment display interface (SITADI). The selected passage shown in green, *MBh.* 12.47.1-3, the beginning of the *Bhīṣmastavarāja* in the *Sāntiparvan* of the *Mahābhārata*, is a link that displays the passage demarcated with red brackets in the manuscript selected in the menu at the top left. Other text annotated in the displayed image appears in blue and other text annotated in the manuscript appears in yellow.

The Sanskrit Library manuscript catalogue's extensive manuscript description apparatus may seem overwhelming; yet the flexibility of digital technology permits data to be accumulated in whatever state it may presently be available. Hence it would be easy to add data available in simpler manuscript lists regardless of how large or small and regardless of how detailed. Small institutions and private

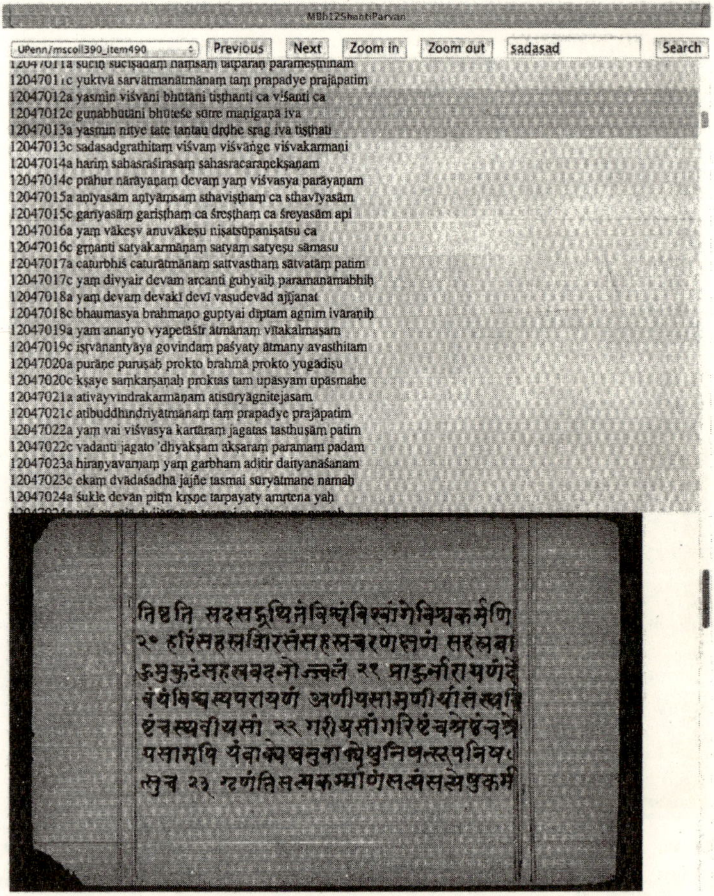

Fig. 13. Image showing the Sanskrit image-text alignment display interface (SITADI) The sought string *sadasad* was located in the passage shown in green, *MBh.* 12.47.13c–16c, in the manuscript shown in the menu at the top left, i.e UPenn Ms. Coll. 390, Item 490. The page of this manuscript linked to the passage in green is shown below.

collections are often overlooked by scholars in their search for manuscripts. The Sanskrit Library is therefore particularly eager to provide centralized access to such minor and private collections.

The Sanskrit Library developed software to convert its TEI manuscript catalogue to the machine readable catalogue format used by most libraries in the U.S. an U.K. (MaRC) and makes the catalogue entries that describe manuscripts available in this form to the libraries that house those manuscripts so that they may be included in standard catalogues at those institutions.

The protocols, formats, and software described above are compatible with web accessible digital images of Sanskrit manuscripts wherever they are hosted. The SITA software is already being used in a project in Kerala, and funneling a new entry through the cataloguing pipeline was recently demonstrated at a workshop in Maharashtra. The Sanskrit Library intends to pursue projects to catalogue and digitize manuscripts at collections of Sanskrit manuscripts nationwide in the U.S. and is eager to collaborate with institutions in India and worldwide to catalogue and digitize manuscripts wherever they may be found.

Appendices

A. Sanskrit Library manuscript cataloguing template

The following are the principal XML elements described by the Text Encoding Initiative's Manuscript Description guidelines included in the Sanskrit Library's manuscript catalogue template:

I. msIdentifier
   A. collection
   B. idno
   C. altIdentifier[type= 'catalog'].collection
   D. altIdentifier[type= 'catalog'].idno
II. msContents
   A. msItemStruct[defective= 'true|false'
   B. rubric
   C. author
   D. title
   E. incipit
   F. explicit
   G. finalRubric
   H. colophon

I. note
   1. persName
   2. title
   3. bibl
J. textLang[mainLang='11-Ssss']

III. physDesc
   A. objectDesc[form='folia|codex']
      1. supportDesc
         a. support.material
         b. extent.measure
         c. extent.dimensions
         d. foliation
         e. foliation.formula
         f. foliation.signatures
         g. collation
         h. collation.formula
         i. condition
      2. layoutDesc
         a. layout
         b. layout[columns]
         c. layout[writtenLines]
   B. handDesc
      1. summary
      2. handNote
   C. decoDesc
      1. decoNote[type= 'color']
      2. decoNote[type= 'border']
      3. decoNote[type= 'illustration']
      4. decoNote[type= 'diagram']
   D. additions
   E. bindingDesc
      1. binding
      2. condition
   F. sealDesc.seal
   G. accMat

IV. history
    A. origin
        1. origDate
        2. persName type= 'scribe|owner'
        3. placeName
        4. geogName
    B. provenance
    C. acquisition
V. additional.adminInfo. recordHist
    A. source
    B. change

B. Sanskrit Library Indic subject classification

I. श्रुति. Aural knowledge, in particular Veda
    A. संहिता. Continuous unalterable text
        1. ऋग्वेद. Collection of verses (*mantra*)
        2. सामवेद. Collection of verses recited in seven tones
        3. यजुर्वेद. Collection of verses and prose
        4. अथर्ववेद. Collection of verses
    B. ब्राह्मण_main. Vedic prose
        1. ब्राह्मण. Prose commentary on ritual and text used in it
        2. आरण्यक. Forest books
        3. उपनिषद्. Private instruction
II. स्मृति. Remembered or traditional knowledge
    A. वेदाङ्ग. Limbs of the Veda
        1. शिक्षा_main. Phonetics
            a. प्रातिशाख्य. Phonetic texts of particular ancient Vedic schools
            b. शिक्षा. Later phonetic treatises
        2. कल्प. Ritual
            a. श्रौतसुत्र. Public ritual
            b. गृह्यसुत्र Domestic ritual
        3. व्याकरण. Grammar
            a. पाणिनीय. Pāṇinian Grammar
            b. अपाणिनीय Non-Pāṇinian Grammar

4. निरुक्त Etymology of Yāska, commentator on Vedic word lists (*nighaṇṭu*)
5. छन्दस्. Metrics, Music
6. ज्योतिष. Astronomy, Astrology

B. दर्शन. Subordinate limbs of veda (*upāṅga*) or philosophical views
   1. न्याय. Epistemology, Logic and Argumentation founded on Gautama's *Nyāyasūtra*
   2. वैषेषिक. Ontology founded on Kaṇāda's *Vaiśeṣikasūtra*
   3. साङ्ख्य. Evolutionary Ontology founded on Kapila's non-extant work
   4. योग. Practice founded on the *Yogasūtra* attributed to Patañjali
   5. कर्ममीमांसा. Ritual Exegesis founded on Jaimini's *Pūrvamīmāṁsāsūtras*
   6. वेदान्त. Metaphysics founded on Bādarāyaṇa's *Uttaramīmāṁsāsūtras*

C. उपवेद. Subordinate Veda
   1. आयुर्वेद Medical Science such as the works of Caraka, Suśruta Vāgbhaṭṭa, etc. (including veterinary medicine and arboriculture)
   2. गन्धर्ववेद_सङ्गीतशास्त्र. Music
   3. धनुर्वेद. Military Science
   4. स्थापत्यवेद_वास्तुशास्त्र. Architecture and Environmental Engineering

D. धर्मशास्त्र. Duty, Custom, and Law
   1. धर्मसूत्र. Rules of particular Vedic schools

E. इतिहास. Narrative, Epic, History
   l. महाभारत. Mahābhārata
   2. रामायण. Rāmāyaṇa

F. पुराण. Ancient Cosmogony, Genealogy, Narrative

III. भक्ति. Devotional literature (including stotras)

IV. तन्त्र. Esoteric ritualism

A. आगम. Authoritative literature in Tantra

B. मन्त्र. Compendia of mantras used in Tantra

V. काव्य. Fine literature and poetry (belles lettres)
VI. कथा. Story literature other than Itihāsa and Purāṇa
VII. कोश. Dictionaries and Thesauri, including nighaṇṭus
VIII. अलङ्कारशास्त्र. Literary criticism
IX. नाट्यशास्त्र. Dance and Theatre
X. शिल्पशास्त्र. Arts and Crafts
XI अर्थशास्त्र. Politics, economics, statecraft (including Nīti)
XII. रत्नशास्त्र. Gemology
XIII. कामशास्त्र. The science of making love
XIV. रसशास्त्र. Alchemy
XV. सङ्ग्रह. Encyclopedias

Contributors

Ashok Kumar Goswami is a Language expert and retired Professor of Sanskrit, Gauhati University. He is presently the Vice-Chairman of Anundoram Barooah Institute of Language. Prof. Goswami is the recipient of "ERDF Excellence Award 2014" given by Education Research & Development Foundation. He has in his credit the books -A Critique of Sabda, Bhavabhuti (Monograph) and many others.

B. N. Goswamy is an Indian art critic, art historian and a former Vice Chairman of the Sarabhai Foundation, Ahmedabad, which runs the Calico Museum of Textiles. Prof. Goswamy is best known for his scholarship on Pahari painting and Indian miniature paintings. He is the author of over twenty books on Arts and Culture, including Sakti Burman: A Private Universe, a monograph on the life and works of Sakti Burman, renowned Bengali painter and *Masters of Indian Painting 1100–1900*, a treatise on Indian miniature art. The Government of India awarded him the Padma Shri in 1998 and followed it up with the Padma Bhushan in 2008.

Dipak Bhattacharya, former Professor of Viswa Bharati University is a well known scholar of Vedic and Linguistic Studies. He was the visiting Professor at many European Universities and has been honoured with many prestigious National and International awards including Collette Caillat Prix of the year 2009 by the Institut de France, Paris.

Over 52 research articles of Prof. Bhattacharya have already been published in National and International Journals. Amongst his various works, the most significant is the critical edition of Paippalāda Samhitā of the Atharvaveda published from Asiatic Society, Kolkata.

Gaya Charan Tripathi (Prof. G. C. Tripathi) is an eminent Indologist. Ph. D. on Vedic deities (Agra), Dr.Phil on Puranic studies (Freiburg/ Germany), D.Litt. on Temple ritual of Orissa (Allahabad). Taught at Freiburg, Aligarh & Udaipur Universities (1967-77), Principal, G.N. Jha Research Institute, Allahabad (1977-2001), Professor and Head of the Kalakosh Division, IGNCA, Delhi (2002-10), Visiting Professor to the Universities of Tuebingen (twice), Leipzig, Berlin, Marburg and British Columbia (twice). National Fellow, Indian Institute of Advanced Studies (2010-12), Presently Director, B.L. Institute of Indology, Delhi.

Peter M. Scharf former professor (Sanskrit), Brown Univeristy, has held several visiting professorships: Visiting Professor at the Maharishi University of Management Research Institute, Chaire Internationale de Recherche Blaise Pascal at the Université Paris Diderot, Visiting Professor in the Department of Sanskrit Studies at the University of Hyderabad, and Visiting Professor in the Department of Humanities and Social Sciences at the Indian Institute of Technology, Bombay. He is also the director of the Sanskrit Library which he founded in 2002. While his research focuses on the linguistic traditions of India, Vedic Sanskrit, and Indian philosophy, he has devoted considerable attention over the past several years to Sanskrit computational linguistics and building a digital Sanskrit library. He is now developing Pāṇinian models of verbal cognition.

Late Sri Pullela Sriramachandrudu was a prolific writer of Sanskrit and Telugu literature. He is best known for translating many difficult Sanskrit works into Telugu including Telugu edition of the Indian epic, Ramayana by Valmiki (seven volume). Prof. Sriramachandrudu, served Sanskrit Academy, Hyderabad from the year 1980 for over a decade and made a mark as a distinguished national scholar. He has been awarded with the Padma Shri by the Government of India in 2011.

Radhavallabh Tripathi is known for his original contributions to literature as well as for his studies on Nāṭyaśāstra and Sāhityaśāstra. Prof. Tripathi has published 162 books, 227 research papers and critical essays. He has received 35 National and International awards and honours for his literary contributions. He has been referred in various research journals on Indology. Research for Ph.D. has been completed as well as is being carried on his creative writings in Sanskrit in a number of universities. Seven books comprising studies on his creative and critical writings by other authors have already been published.

Rama Nath Sharma, a traditional Sanskrit scholar is Currently Emeritus professor of Sanskrit at the University of Hawaii, USA. Prof. Sharma is internationally known for his lectures on, studies in, the aṣṭādhyāyī of Pāṇini and Sanskrit intellectual tradition. He travelled to all major institutions of higher learning in India, lecturing on Panini as a Fullbright Scholar (2005). He has presented papers, chaired sessions, and delivered key note addresses at many National and International conferences.

Prof. Sharma's *The Aṣṭādhyāyī of Pāṇini* (six volumes in English) is a significant contribution to the scholarly world.

Som Prakash Verma taught at the Centre of Advanced Study, Department of History, Aligarh Muslim University and was the Tagore National Fellow (2010–12). At present, he is Senior Academic Fellow at the Indian Council of Historical Research, New Delhi.